,15.

Ber

Lanzarote &

ARTIZAN ST. LIBRARY
05/15

Fuerteventura

TOP 10 ATTRACTIONS

Teguise • The former capital of Lanzarote is an attractive town that holds a busy market every Sunday *(page 46)*

Fuerteventura's windmills • A reminder of a time before tourism *(page 71)*

Timanfaya • An unforgettable volcanic landscape *(page 54)*

Betancuria • Cobbled streets and courtyards in a pretty 15th century town *(page 72)*

ájara • A red sandstone doorway adorns the church in this picturesque village *(page 75)*

Costa Calma • Sweeps of white sand draw visitors to Fuerteventura's Sotavento beaches *(page 77)*

l Jable dunes • These great mpty swathes of sand lie ust outside lively Corralejo n northern Fuerteventura *page 69)*

Fundación César Manrique • The former home of Lanzarote's iconic artist and architect *(page 43)*

ueva de los Verdes • Take a rip through the dramatic va-formed caves *(page 36)*

Puerto del Carmen • Lanzarote's biggest resort offers some of the island's best beaches *(page 51)*

A PERFECT TOUR

Day 1   Beach day

Spend the day exploring your base, Puerto del Carmen. Stroll along the attractive promenade, find a good spot to laze on Playa Grande, then enjoy a late fishy lunch at La Lonja (Calle Varadero).

Day 3   Arrecife and the Fundación Manrique

Visit the island capital, Arrecife, to explore the backstreets and have coffee by the Charco (lagoon). Then head to the Fundación César Manrique, a splendid museum and gallery in what was the artist's home, with murals, paintings, ceramics and views over the eerie volcanic landscape.

Day 4   Teguise

Head to Teguise when it is not market day (Sunday), so you can enjoy the pretty streets, admire the ornate colonial buildings and have lunch in the Patio del Vino (Calle Herrera y Rojas). Just outside town, visit the hilltop Castillo de Santa Bárbara for stunning views and the fascinating Museum of Immigration.

Day 2   The island interior

Drive through La Geria wine country, stopping at Bodega El Grifo to sample wine and explore the museum, then head towards the Monumento del Campesino in the centre of the island. Visit the adjoining artisan centre, then time your return journey to include an early (pre-booked) dinner (from 8pm) at the stunning La Tegala in Macher.

OF LANZAROTE

Day 6 Mirador del Río and Isla Graciosa

Not far from Haría is the Parque Tropical, with exotic birds and subtropical plants. Continue to the far north of the island for lunch at the café at the Mirador del Río, from where there are spectacular views. You should have time for the short boat trip from nearby Orzola to Isla Graciosa, a completely undeveloped little island.

Day 5 To the north

Book a night's accommodation in Haría, an arty little town in the verdant 'Valley of a Thousand Palms'. Go first to the extraordinary underground world of the Jameos del Agua (another Manrique creation) then return to Haría for a late lunch at Dos Hermanos (Plaza León y Castillo).

Day 8 Papagayo

Drive to Playa Blanca at the far south of the island. Stroll around this pretty resort and buy food for a picnic, then take the *Princesa Yaiza* glass-bottomed boat from the harbour for a 45-minute trip to the beautiful, and protected, Papagayo beaches.

Day 7 Parque Nacional de Timanfaya

Back at Puerto del Carmen, drive via the idyllic village of Yaiza to the Parque Nacional de Timanfaya. Go for a camel ride at the Echado de Camellos then take a tour around the Montañas del Fuego, before eating meat grilled over natural volcanic heat at El Diablo restaurant.

Map labels: Teguise · 404 · Teseguitel · Castillo de St Bárbara y Museo del Emigrante · Nazaret · St Bárbara · Punta de Tierra Negra · Costa Teguise · Playa de los Charcos · Playa de las Cucharas · Playa del Tío Joaquín · Pu... · de C...

CONTENTS

60

101

93

INTRODUCTION

Swept by trade winds and warmed by coastal currents, the islands of Lanzarote and Fuerteventura offer a consistently warm climate, with some 300 days of sunshine a year. They are part of the Canary Islands, which lie approximately 1,100km (690 miles) southwest of the Spanish mainland and, at the nearest point, 115km (70 miles) from the West African coast. Although part of Spain, in 1982 the islands became an autonomous province, divided in two: the eastern islands, which include Lanzarote and Fuerteventura, are governed by a Cabildo Insular (Island Council) from Las Palmas de Gran Canaria, the western islands from Santa Cruz de Tenerife.

Lanzarote is some 60km (38 miles) in length and 24km (15 miles) across at its widest point, with a population of about 116,000, of whom some 48,000 live in the capital, Arrecife. Fuerteventura is larger, at around 100km (60 miles) long and 30km (18 miles) wide, but sparsely populated – there are around 79,000 inhabitants, of whom about half live in Puerto del Rosario.

Landscape and Climate

The whole volcanic archipelago is barren, but Lanzarote and Fuerteventura are drier and more barren than the rest. Lanzarote's last volcanic explosion was in 1824, but the heat is still close to the surface, as you will find if you go to the Parque Nacional Timanfaya, and much of the island is still covered with cindery *malpaís* (badlands). Fuerteventura has seen no volcanic activity for some 5,000 years, but has less rain than any of the islands, and the landscape is coloured in shades of brown and khaki, with great expanses of dunes.

Charco de San Ginés lagoon in Arrecife

Playa Blanca, a beach at the resort with the same name

Lanzarote's highest point is Montaña Blanca, at 670m (2,198ft). The beaches around the major resorts, especially the famous ones at Puerto del Carmen, are covered with golden sands, as are the beautiful stretches close to Playa Blanca, while smaller, rockier coves retain their black volcanic sand. Of Fuerteventura's 152 beaches, some 50km (32 miles) consist of white sand, while about 25km (15 miles) are black volcanic shingle. The highest point on the island is Monte Jandía (807m/2,648ft).

The islands' average annual temperature is 20°C (68°F), soaring in high summer to 28–30°C (82–86°F). Fuerteventura is usually windy – one explanation for the island's name is that it comes from *viento fuerte* (strong wind). On both islands, early mornings can be cloudy before blue skies and sunshine take over. There is little rain – what there is falls mostly between October and January. In summer the islands sometimes suffer from what is known as *tiempo Africano*

(African weather), when the hot sirocco wind sweeps up from the Sahara, covering the landscape with reddish dust.

Vegetation and Farming

There are few trees, apart fom the Canary palms *(Phoenix Canariensis)* in the Haría Valley, and those planted along the roadsides of many towns and resorts. Parks, hotel grounds and botanical gardens are bright with exotic plants brought to the island from southern Africa, South America and elsewhere that flourish happily in the islands' subtropical climate. The Strelitzia (bird-of-paradise flower) is one of the most showy, but hibiscus, poinsettia and agave are also common, and vividly coloured bougainvillea rampages over the garden walls and facades of villas and hotels.

Various forms of *Euphorbia* (spurge) flourish on the scrubby soil, including the *Euphorbia Canariensis* (candelabra spurge) and the rare, cactus-like *cardón de Jandía (Euphorbia handiensis)*, found in the south of Fuerteventura.

A variety of prickly pear cactus cultivated mainly on Lanzarote is the nopal, on which the cochineal beetle feeds. When crushed, the beetle produces a red dye – cochineal. This is not the lucrative industry it was in the 19th century *(see page 18)*, but a recent resurgence of interest in natural products means cochineal is being produced in Lanzarote, but on a much smaller scale.

Another form of vegetation is that produced on the

Aloe vera

On both islands you will see aloe vera, another cactus-like plant that has become very popular for medicinal and cosmetic purposes – especially to soothe sunburn – and is being widely cultivated. The plant has long, greyish-green spiky leaves and spears of yellow flowers. You will find the products for sale in small shops, markets and supermarkets all over the islands.

Cacti flourish in the islands' dry, sandy soil

black lava called *picón*. This cinder, which collects and stores moisture from dew, is spread over arid soil and used for the cultivation of vines – especially in the La Geria region.

Wildlife

There is plenty for bird-watchers to spot on both islands in winter. Lanzarote's central plain is the best place to see Houbara bustards, kestrels, stone curlews and trumpeter finches – which are also found on Fuerteventura, along with the Fuerteventura chat. Berthelot's pipit can be seen all over the island, hoopoes are fairly common, and chiffchaffs and warblers are often found in urban settings. The Salinas de Janubio (salt pans) are a stopping-off place for many migratory birds, and numerous seabirds cluster on the offshore islands.

There are few mammals on either island: bats, rats, mice, squirrels, rabbits and hedgehogs are about the sum of it. There are reptiles, though: geckos and lizards. The water around the islands is home to dolphins, porpoises and whales, and is rich in fish, including *corvina* (a kind of sea bass), *cherne* (wreckfish or stone bass), *sama* (sea bream) and *vieja* (parrot fish), as well as more homely *sardinas* (sardines).

People and Language

The people of the Canary Islands have a strong sense of their identity as islanders and are keen to stress that they are *canarios* first and foremost. Spanish *(castellano)* is the language of the islands, but there are subtle differences from the peninsula, many of which reflect the two-way traffic between the Canaries and Latin America. Final consonants are swallowed and 'z' is pronounced 's', as in the Americas, rather than the lisped 'th' of mainland Spain. A number of Latino words have been borrowed, too: a bus is a *guagua* and potatoes are *papas*.

The Impact of Tourism

Traditionally, the islands' economy has been dependent on agriculture, but the principal source of revenue today comes from tourism. Lanzarote and Fuerteventura lack the loud nightlife and laddish culture that typifies parts of Tenerife and Gran Canaria. The strong winds and good waves attract surfing enthusiasts, but, apart from this, the equable climate means that the islands are all-round holiday destinations, with many older northern European visitors favouring the

Traditional costumes and music at a Lanzarote fiesta

cooler months as an escape from their own harsher winters, while families are in the majority during school holidays.

Obviously, the influx of tourists has had a major impact on the character of the islands, although Lanzarote has escaped the high-rise desecration that has spoiled parts of Tenerife and Gran Canaria. This is due in large part to the vision of artist César Manrique *(see page 27)*, who was influential in persuading the authorities to work with the island's landscape and natural features. Fuerteventura, which came later to tourism, has some rather characterless new resorts, but on the whole they are not badly done.

The resort of Caleta de Fuste on Fuerteventura

From volcanic landscapes to sandy beaches, the islands have much to offer, whether visitors are looking for water sports or family entertainment, or are keen to discover the island way of life. The islands are easy to get around on well-surfaced roads, and there are some pleasant walking routes to suit people of all ages. While most accommodation is in purpose-built complexes, *turismo rural* has gained a foothold, making it possible to stay in rural properties in beautiful surroundings *(see page 135)* and sample traditional food. All in all, enough to convince most people that the islands merit one of their early names – the Fortunate Isles.

A BRIEF HISTORY

The Canary Islands have been part of Spain since they were conquered in the late 15th century, but there was a flourishing culture here long before that, although no one is quite sure where the pre-Hispanic people came from. These early inhabitants are known collectively as the Guanches, although strictly speaking this was the name of a tribe that inhabited Tenerife. The people of Lanzarote and Fuerteventura prefer the name Majoreros, which is derived from Fuerteventura's indigenous name – Maxorata. Some historians think the original inhabitants were related to the Canarii people, who lived on the Saharan side of the Atlas Mountains. But as far as we know, the Guanches had no boats, so how they crossed from the African coast remains a mystery.

The Guanches (or Majoreros) were an agricultural people who mostly lived in groups of caves, but on the three eastern islands they also built houses. On Lanzarote and Fuerteventura their dwellings were grouped into hamlets around the edges of lava fields. Their society had a hierarchical structure, with kings – *guanartemes* – and priests – *faycans*. Lanzarote was a single kingdom, but on Fuerteventura there were two – Maxorata in the north and Jandía in the south, beyond La Pared, the wall that once stretched across the narrowest part of the island. These early people mummified their dead and buried them in caves or stone-lined graves, and it is evidence from mummies that has led scientists to place the islanders' ethnic origins in northwest Africa.

The Guanches did not have the wheel, they knew nothing of metalworking and did not use bows and arrows – their main weapons were wooden spears. Domestic implements were made from stone and bone or from obsidian, a black, volcanic glass. Porous lava was made into millstones and

Marital custom

Scientist and explorer Alexander von Humboldt, who visited Lanzarote in 1799 en route to South America, claimed the indigenous people had an unusual custom: 'A woman had several husbands, who each took it in turn to exercise the rights of the head of the family. Each husband was known as such during a lunar month; then another took his place while he returned to being a servant in the house.'

mortars. Their vessels and containers were made from pottery, wood, leather and woven cane. *Gofio*, toasted flour originally made from barley, was their staple food, but they also ate a variety of roots, wild fruits and berries. Pigs, sheep and goats provided meat as well as the materials for shelters, containers and clothes, and milk also came from sheep and goats. Fish formed a part of their diet, even when they had to travel some distance down to the coast to find it.

Arrival of the Europeans

The first documented account of a European expedition to the Canary Islands was in 1339, when the Genoese Lanzarotto Malocello discovered the island that was named after him. The first detailed description of the islands was written two years later by Genoese historian Nicoloso da Recco, who accompanied a slave-traders' voyage. He wrote: 'The natives of Fuerteventura are few in number and live on meat and milk, and are of great stature, and are very firm in their beliefs.' Various expeditions were mounted during the course of the century, but it was not until 1402 that the first conquerors arrived. Jean de Béthencourt and Gadifer de la Salle, Norman noblemen who had pledged allegiance to the king of Castile, claimed Lanzarote, Fuerteventura and El Hierro for their royal master, but failed to take Gran Canaria and Tenerife. Like most conquerors, they claimed the expedition was 'for the exaltation of the Christian faith', so they must have been delighted when the last king of Lanzarote, after several failed escape attempts, agreed to Christian baptism.

Many of the indigenous people were sold into slavery and many more died of European diseases, but those who survived intermarried with the colonisers, who settled down to a harsh life, making their living from the land and sea.

It was not until 1478 that another attempt was made to conquer the two larger islands, under the aegis of Ferdinand and Isabella – the so-called Catholic Monarchs of a newly united Spain. It took several years to subdue the indigenous people, but eventually all the Canary Islands became Spanish possessions.

Because of their location, the islands were vital for Spanish colonisation in the Americas. This revolved around slavery and sugar cane, both of which were introduced to the Americas from the Canaries, but it was Gran Canaria and Tenerife that were the main beneficiaries. Of no interest to their Spanish masters and with little source of income, many inhabitants of Lanzarote and Fuerteventura turned to piracy during the 16th and early 17th centuries, a somewhat precarious way of earning a living, and one that laid them open to reciprocal attacks.

Jean de Béthencourt

Explosive Events

During the mid-18th century, memories of pirate raids faded into insignificance when Lanzarote experienced a disastrous series of volcanic eruptions. In 1730, Volcán Timanfaya erupted, and continued to pour molten lava and black ash down its slopes for a further six years, until a third of the island had been devastated, many of its inhabitants had fled to Gran Canaria and some had set out on the long journey to Latin America. For almost a century the volcano appeared to sleep, but 1824 saw another series of eruptions, albeit smaller ones. Visitors to the dark, eerie landscape now protected as the Parque Nacional de Timanfaya may be able to visualise the devastation.

Although the eruptions overwhelmed the most fertile part of the island, the volcanic ash formed *picón*, dark cinders that collect and retain the dew, forming a natural irrigation system. On this the islanders were able to grow a variety of vegetables, and to profit from the cultivation of vines and the export of wine, ushering in a period of prosperity that lasted until the early years of the 19th century. This system, known as *enarenad*, was later practised in arid parts of the Spanish mainland, although silicon sand was used instead of cinder.

The next money-spinner was cochineal, a red dye created by crushing the beetle (*Dactylopius coccus costa*) that fed on the nopal cactus, and which was introduced to the islands in around 1825. For some 50 years the

Mountain of fire

The parish priest of Yaiza, Andrés Lorenzo Curbelo, described the 1730 eruption as 'an enormous mountain that rose out of the bosom of the earth. From its flat top flames belched out and continued burning for 19 days'. Several months later 'new eruptions came... [with] incandescent streams of lava, together with the densest smoke'.

Volcanic landscape formed by the eruptions of Timanfaya

industry flourished, before the creation of aniline dyes made it largely superfluous.

During the latter part of this period the larger, more powerful islands of Gran Canaria and Tenerife were flexing their muscles, demanding a degree of independence from Spain and vying with each other for supremacy at the same time. Tenerife, which had profited from the wine trade (Gran Canaria's soil was unsuitable for viniculture) and other long-distance commerce was by far the wealthier and had established a university in the town of La Laguna, which became an intellectual centre. Gran Canaria resented Tenerife's powerful position and, under the late 19th-century leadership of Fernando León y Castillo, foreign minister in the national government, made a bid for supremacy.

In 1903, emboldened by Cuba gaining freedom from Spain five years earlier, the Partido Local Canario was formed, with the aim of achieving some degree of independence and dividing the archipelago into two provinces. This was formalised in 1927, but brought little economic relief to the islands, whose trade had been badly hit by World War I and its economic aftermath. Lanzarote and Fuerteventura became part of the Eastern Province, governed, as they are today, from Las Palmas de Gran Canaria. The seat of island government (Cabildo Insular) alternates between Las Palmas and Santa Cruz de Tenerife every four years.

There had been a steady flow of people from the Canaries to the Americas since the late 16th century, but agricultural decline in the late 19th and early 20th centuries increased this traffic, as people went looking for a better way of life. Remittances were sent home, and many of those who made good returned to the islands and built homes or established small businesses, thus accentuating the ties with Latin America that are still apparent today. You can visit

Many *canarios* emigrated to the Americas

the Museo del Emigrante just outside Teguise (Lanzarote) to learn more about this *(see page 48)*.

Political Upheavals

In 1924, under the dictatorship of Miguel Primo de Rivera, Fuerteventura, the bleakest of the Canary Islands, was judged a suitable place to send political

dissidents. Writer and philosopher Miguel de Unamuno was the best known of these. He came to love the island, which he described as 'a rock thirsting in the sun, a treasure of health and honesty'. There is a monument to him in the north of the island.

In 1936, the three-year Spanish Civil War began, initiated by Francisco Franco, military governor of the Canary Islands. He spent the last night before launching his coup in the Hotel Madrid in Las Palmas.

After the bitter Civil War and World War II, the Canaries, like the rest of Spain, initially suffered from political isolation and economic hardship. Things improved a little in the 1950s, when Spain was once more recognised by the international community, but it was the advent of tourism in the following decade that really turned the tide.

Franco remained in power until his death in 1975, when his authoritarian regime was replaced by democratic government. The new Spanish Constitution of 1978 created the Autonomous Region of the Canary Islands – now one of 17 such regions. The archipelago is not completely separate from Spain, but the island government, the Cabildo Insular, does have a great deal of freedom.

Many people have swapped agricultural work for jobs in resorts

In the national elections of 1996, the Coalición Canaria, a union of regional parties, took four seats in the Madrid parliament (reduced to three in 2004 and two in 2008). It now sees its role as working with the national government to win improvements for the islands, rather than looking for further independence. This is not to say that no resentment is felt towards Madrid, but resentment of central government is, perhaps, a fact of life wherever regional feelings are strong.

Many mainland Spaniards, particularly from the poorer regions – Andalusia and Galicia – are to be found working in the islands' service industries. They have integrated well into island life and, while there is some dissatisfaction expressed about them doing jobs that might be done by local people, there is relatively little ill-feeling.

The islands have enjoyed considerable commercial freedom and tax exemptions ever since the 19th century. When Spain became a full member of the European Union, fiscal changes had to be introduced, but important tax privileges were negotiated. Motorists will be pleased to find that, in a period of rocketing fuel prices, the islands still have the cheapest petrol in Europe.

Tourism, Economy and Environment

Traditionally, the economy of the islands has been dependent on agriculture and fishing, but the principal source of employment and revenue today is in the service sector, of which tourism is a major part. Some 90 percent of Lanzarote's inhabitants work in the tourist industry and the infrastructure that supports it, and the percentage in Fuerteventura is similar. When Arrecife airport opened in the early 1960s (it was refurbished and extended in 1999 to cope with the large number of passengers), tourism started to take off. Fuerteventura's airport opened in 1969, and while the growth of the tourist industry was slower here than on the other islands, it has increased in recent years. Lanzarote now receives about 1.8 million visitors annually, Fuerteventura some 1.5 million, mainly English, Germans and Scandinavians, as well as visitors from mainland Spain. Despite the widespread

Dangerous Journeys

Lanzarote and Fuerteventura have become the main route into Europe for illegal immigrants from Africa now that strict controls have made it more difficult for them to cross from northern Morocco to southern Spain. Desperate people, many from war-torn sub-Saharan regions, pay traffickers up to €1,200 (around £1,000) to reach the Moroccan coast, where they are loaded onboard small, ill-equipped boats to make the dangerous journey to these islands, which are the closest to the African coast. Many drown, or die of dehydration, during the course of their journey. Others reach the island shores to face an uncertain future.

economic downturn, tourist figures on the islands are holding up well. There are believed to be around 50,000 foreign property owners on Lanzarote, and some have established bars, clubs and other small businesses. There are fewer home owners on Fuerteventura, but numbers are rising.

The eastern islands suffer from severe water shortage (they receive less rainfall than parts of the Sahara), a problem intensified by the strain that so many visitors place on the system. The creation of desalination plants has helped, but visitors should try to be frugal in their use of water, although in hot summer weather it can be rather difficult.

Turbines utilise the strong winds the islands receive

The availability of work in the tourist industry has encouraged many young people to desert the land and the fishing industry (although Arrecife still has the biggest fishing fleet in the Canaries) in favour of higher wages and more fun in the resorts. But life for the islanders has rarely been easy, and it is understandable that the latest generation should look for alternatives. Most people believe that tourism has brought more advantages than disadvantages to the islands, and that the inhabitants' individuality and love of their lands will enable them to retain their special character, despite the many changes.

Historical Landmarks

c.2nd–1st centuries BC Settlements of Guanches in Canary Islands.
AD1339 Genoese Lanzarotto Malocello discovers Lanzarote.
1402 Jean de Béthencourt and Gadifer de la Salle invade and claim Lanzarote, Fuerteventura and El Hierro.
1478–83 Canary Islands brought under control of Spanish Crown.
16th–17th centuries Many inhabitants of impoverished Lanzarote and Fuerteventura turn to piracy.
1730–6 Continuous eruptions of Mount Timanfaya; a third of Lanzarote is devastated.
1730–1950 Poverty forces widespread emigration to Latin America.
1825–75 Economic boom follows the introduction of the cochineal beetle, but the industry is ruined by the invention of aniline dyes.
1852 Isabella II declares the Canary Islands a Free Trade Zone.
1911 Self-administration council – Cabildo Insular – introduced.
1927 Canary Islands are divided in two. Lanzarote and Fuerteventura become part of the Eastern Province, governed from Gran Canaria.
1936 Franco initiates the three-year Spanish Civil War.
1962 Lanzarote's Arrecife airport opens. Tourism rapidly develops into the most important industry.
1969 Fuerteventura airport opens. Tourism develops more slowly here.
1970s Influenced by artist and architect César Manrique, the Cabildo imposes strict building regulations on Lanzarote.
1978–82 Spanish Constitution joins the two island provinces to form the Autonomous Region of the Canary Islands.
1986 Spain joins the EU and negotiates special status for the Canaries.
1995 Islands integrated into the EU but retain important tax privileges.
2002 The euro becomes the national currency.
2005–6 Lanzarote receives about 1.8 million visitors annually, Fuerteventura some 1.5 million.
2010 Tourist numbers remain stable despite economic downturn.
2011 In regional elections the right-of-centre PP and the Coalición Canaria both gained seats at the expense of the left-wing PSOE.

LANZAROTE

L anzarote is a small island, but it packs a lot of contrasts into a limited space. From the awesome, unearthly Montañas del Fuego in the Parque Nacional de Timanfaya to the verdant 'Valley of a Thousand Palms' around Haría; from the tranquillity of Isla Graciosa to the razzmatazz of Puerto del Carmen, there is always something to surprise the visitor. One thing is consistent, however: the building limits proposed by artist César Manrique and imposed by the island government have ensured that, with a few exceptions, the architecture consists of low white buildings with green, blue or brown balconies and shutters, which complement the indigenous architecture of the island.

Lanzarote is an easy place to get around. For the sake of simplicity this guide starts with the capital, Arrecife, then divides the island into three areas: north, south and centre. However, distances are so small that you may find yourself straying from one region to the other on a single trip. Just follow your own instincts and you won't go far wrong.

ARRECIFE

Arrecife lies 8km (5 miles) east of the airport, from where it is well served by inexpensive taxis. Buses *(guaguas)* run every 20 minutes to Costa Teguise and Puerto del Carmen, and taxi fares to both resorts are very reasonable. The town has a long history, as its two sturdy fortresses demonstrate. Castillo de San Gabriel was built in the second half of the 17th century to reinforce the town against attacks from the sea; it was the work of Genoese engineer Leonardo Torriani,

One of Playa Blanca's inviting beaches

who also built Teguise's Castillo de Santa Bárbara. The Castillo de San José dates from about a century later, when pirate attacks were still a problem. It was also a work-creation project, as the islanders were suffering great poverty following periods of drought and the eruption of Timanfaya, which had destroyed farmland in the most fertile part of the island. For a long time it was known as the Castillo del Hambre (Fortress of Hunger). In 1852, when piracy had ceased to be a threat, and links with Spain's American colonies meant that it made more sense to have a capital on the coast, Arrecife took over from Teguise as the capital of Lanzarote.

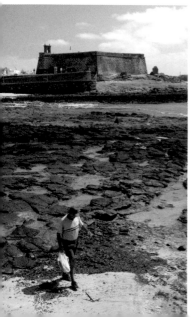

Crossing the shore in front of Castillo de San Gabriel

Arrecife is a down-to-earth, working city, home to almost half the island's population. It has few buildings of architectural interest and not a great deal in the way of culture, but it is well worth a visit to see a slice of island life, away from the resorts or the picture-postcard villages. It has a few decent tapas bars, an excellent restaurant in the Castillo de San José, food to be purchased in the market and local shops that is cheaper and more varied than in the resorts, and an excellent curved beach – Playa Reducto – with golden sands and calm, safe waters. If you want a quiet holiday there is a lot to be said for making a base here in one of the seafront hotels.

Exploring the Town

If you come to Arrecife by car, get off the *circunvalación* (ring road) at the west (airport) end of town, where you can park in a large car park at the end of the beach, opposite the smart new Cabildo Insular building, and thereby avoid

Quiosco de la Música

the narrow streets and one-way system of the city. Looming at the other end of the beach is the 17-storey **Gran Hotel** (which has a large underground car park). This was the building that so upset Manrique when he returned from New York that he took steps to ensure that Lanzarote's skyline would not become disfigured by similar high-rises. The hotel was gutted by fire in 1994 and remained empty for years but reopened in 2004. Although it breaks all the rules, it is a sleek, well-designed building. Take the glass lift to the top, where a there's a restaurant and a café that offers views over the town and down to Puerto del Carmen – and good coffee and cake.

Newly planted gardens and a wooden walkway lead towards the town centre. On a corner, opposite an attractive Canarian-style building belonging to the Cabildo, old men sit in a little square playing dominoes. A broad promenade runs east from here. The statue at the beginning is of Blas Cabrera Felipe (1878–1945), an eminent scientist who was born in the town. There are seats in flower-decked bowers, and egrets squawk and flap in the palm trees. The circular wooden **Quiosco de la Música**, where a band sometimes

Charco de San Ginés

plays, also serves as the town's tourist information office. On the other side of the road, the Avenida de la Marina, is the post office and the **Casa de Cultura Agustín de la Hoz** (Mon–Fri 10am–5pm; charge) in which early murals by César Manrique were discovered during the course of renovation.

Cross a little bridge to the **Castillo de San Gabriel** (Tue–Fri 10am–1pm, 4–7pm, Sat 10am–1pm; free), with a rusty cannon standing outside. The sturdy little fortress houses a small ethnographic and archaeological museum, with information about the Guanches (or Majoreros), the island's original inhabitants, but it will not detain you for long. You can cross back to the seafront via a parallel bridge, the **Puente de las Bolas**, named for the cannon balls atop its twin pillars. Follow the promenade (now called Avenida Coll) a short way to the right (towards the port), passing the Ayuntamiento (Town Hall), then cross the road to the **Charco de San Ginés**. This pretty little tidal lagoon, where boats bob serenely on the water, is surrounded by brightly shuttered buildings, several of which house restaurants. The only incongruous feature is a large, four-screen cinema (Multicines Atlántida) but local people are probably glad of the entertainment.

You can walk all the way round the lagoon then off into the town to the Plaza de las Palmas, and the parish church, the **Iglesia de San Ginés** (daily 9am–1pm, 4–7pm), with a distinctive white cupola topping its bell tower. It is dedicated to the town's patron saint, whose festival is celebrated here in August. There is a simple interior, with a good Mudéjar ceiling of dark wood. If you find the church closed (the opening hours are not to be relied on), just sit on one of the benches in the shady square, listen to the drip of a central fountain and admire the exterior of the building.

Narrow lanes lead from the square into the centre of the town, focused on the pedestrianised shopping street, **Calle León y Castillo**, running back from the seafront. Here, branches of well-known stores such as Zara and Mango share space with the large HiperDino supermarket and a few delightfully old-fashioned shops such as the Almacenes Arencibia, with shirts and jerseys stacked neatly on glass-fronted wooden shelves.

Art in Arrecife
Go west, via the oblong Plaza de la Constitución – where there are a couple of tapas bars with seats outside in the square – towards Calle Betancort. Here (No. 33) you will find **El Almacén** (Mon–Fri 10am–2pm, 7pm–midnight; free), a ◄Ⓒ

León y Castillo

You may wonder why most towns and villages in Lanzarote have a street or square called León y Castillo. This has nothing to do with lions or castles, but pays homage to two brothers, Fernando and Juan, who were born in Telde, Gran Canaria, where there is now a museum devoted to them. Fernando, who became foreign minister in the Spanish government in 1881, implemented a programme of improvements to the port of Las Palmas, the plans for which were drawn up by his engineer brother Juan. This made it the major port in the archipelago and an important stop on the new steamship route to the West Indies, and changed the ailing fortunes of Gran Canaria and, by extension, of Lanzarote and Fuerteventura.

Castillo de San José

cultural centre in an old store converted by César Manrique. The centre includes the Bar Picasso, where there is sometimes live music, two galleries with changing exhibitions and, on the top floor, the Cine Buñuel, which screens art house films.

Arrecife is a small town, and all of the above can easily be done on foot, but to visit the last place of interest you need to take a taxi. They are readily available, and it should cost no more than €5 from the centre to the **Castillo de San José**, which houses the **Museo Internacional de Arte Contemporáneo** (daily 11am–9pm; free). The fortress had fallen into disrepair by the 20th century, and in 1975 Manrique directed the renovation of the building and founded the Museum of Contemporary Art. In a series of cool rooms within the thick stone walls is a collection of paintings, sketches and sculpture by internationally known artists such as Antoni Tàpies, as well as Manrique himself and other renowned Canarian artists.

Down a flight of stairs more paintings decorate the walls of a restaurant and bar (daily 11am–midnight). From the floor-to-ceiling windows there is a view of the new Puerto de los Mármoles – not traditionally picturesque, but in this context the cranes, ships and containers have a sculptural beauty. You can eat very well here *(see page 106)*, or just enjoy the view from a low, comfy bar stool while you have a drink – and bar prices are surprisingly low for such a smart venue.

THE NORTH

The north of the island is a treasure trove of natural wonders and man-made attractions. Nature has given us the dramatic cliffs of Risco de Famara on the west coast, the *malpaís* (badlands) on the east, the fascinating Cueva de los Verdes and the tranquil island of Isla Graciosa, while man (or, to be specific, Manrique) has created the breathtaking Jameos del Agua, the Jardín de Cactus and the Mirador del Río.

Jardín de Cactus and Arrieta

From the *circunvalación* around Arrecife, take the LZ1 north towards **Guatiza** to visit the **Jardín de Cactus** (daily 10am–5.45pm; charge includes a drink in the café). As you enter Guatiza you pass fields of cultivated cactus, for this is the region where cochineal is still produced, albeit not in large quantities *(see page 18)*. Set in a volcanic crater, this Manrique-designed garden spirals in a circle of terraces up to a small windmill. There are cacti of all kinds: round and dumpy, tall and phallic, and some like little furry creatures snuggled in the volcanic soil. Manrique's designs on the external walls of the toilets are attractions in themselves.

Jardín de Cactus

A sad tale

A strange house stands on one of Arrieta's jetties, pagoda-like in bright blue and brick-red. The building has a sad story to tell: in the 1920s a local man emigrated to Argentina, where he prospered, but his young daughter fell gravely ill and he was advised that the Atlantic winds would be good for her. He returned and built a house as exposed to the elements as possible in a style popular in Argentina. Sadly, the daughter died, despite his care, and is buried in the local cemetery.

En route from Guatiza to the Jameos del Agua, you could make a brief detour to **Arrieta**. We are in Manrique country here, and one of his sculptures, like a giant wind chime, stands at a roundabout where a road leads the short distance to this tiny fishing village. To the right, before you enter the village, you could turn off to the pleasant **Playa de la Garita**. Arrieta is a sleepy place, although popular with divers, and it gets animated at weekend lunch times when several fish restaurants around the small harbour draw customers. Also worth a visit is the **Aloe Vera House** (Calle Cortijo 2; Mon–Sat 10am–6pm; free), which has lots of information on the production and uses of the plant.

Jameos del Agua and Cueva de los Verdes

Continue north for 3km (2 miles) to the well-signposted **Jameos del Agua** (tel: 928 848 020; daily 10am–6.30pm, Tue–Sat also 7pm–2am; restaurant 7–11.30pm; charge). You turn off onto a road that is in many places not wide enough for two-way traffic, but there are many passing places, and people are usually courteous about using them. This is one site that just about everybody comes to, so it can get busy – try to come fairly early, or at the end of the day – and it is like nothing else you will ever have seen. It is part of a volcanic tunnel system that runs from Montaña de Corona, which erupted about 4,000 years ago, out into the Atlantic. It was this eruption that created the *malpaís* (now a protected area) through which you will drive if you continue north. A *jameo* is the name for a cavity produced when the roof of a volcanic tunnel collapses.

Within this one, Manrique created an extraordinary underground world. You go down steps to the *jameo chico* (small cave) to a bar/restaurant, full of lush foliage and soft music, from where narrow paths lead to a saltwater lake of varying depth depending on the tide. The lake is home to a unique variety of crab *(Munidopsis polymorpha)*, white, blind and without shells – as they have no predators, they had no need to develop them. Notices around the lake (and on your ticket) tell you that it is forbidden to throw coins into the water, as their corrosion would endanger the crabs. At the other side of the lake, landscaped terraces lead up

At the Jameos del Agua

Cueva de los Verdes

to ground level. At the far side is a 600-seat auditorium, with splendid acoustics; closed for renovation for some years, it reopened for performances in 2008.

About 1km (½ mile) up a narrow road opposite lies the **Cueva de los Verdes** ◄ **5** (daily 10am–6pm, last entry 5pm; guided tour; charge; www.lanzarote.com/cueva-de-los-verdes). *Verde* means green, but the name refers not to the colour of the rocks but to a family called Verde who used to keep goats in the upper part of the cave. Over the years, these caverns served as a place of refuge for local people when pirates attacked. The cave system is part of the same 'tube' that runs from Montaña de Corona to the sea.

You may have to wait a short while to go in as the numbers on each 50-minute tour are limited; however, they run very frequently. The temperature inside the caves remains at 18–20°C (64–68°F) throughout the year, which makes the visit a pleasant escape from summer heat. Claustrophobics should be all right, as, after an initial low, narrow stretch, the cave opens out into a vast cavern, and thereafter there are few places where you need to stoop. The tour does involve shuffling along rather slowly, however – how slowly depends on the composition of your group and how many people linger to take photos. It's worth the shuffle, though, as the shapes of the cave walls and ceilings, formed by the solidified lava and enhanced by discreet lighting, are extraordinary. Your guide will lead you into an auditorium, where concerts are sometimes held, as the acoustics are excellent. As the tour draws to an end, the guide will demand silence in order to introduce you to the 'secret of the caves' – it's an ingenious one, and we are not going to give the game away.

Mirador del Río and Parque Tropical

Continue north, through cindery *malpaís*, where only lichen-covered rocks and euphorbia bushes enliven the black terrain. After a while a few small vineyards appear, the vines planted in the traditional Lanzarote way, within a semicircle of rocks *(see page 51)*. On a hillside, a bodega offers tastings and sells wine. The road ends at the **Mirador del Río** (daily 10am–6pm; charge). You will not be surprised to learn that it was Manrique who transformed this disused gun emplacement into a lookout point and glass-fronted café. The views are stupendous, encompassing Isla

The view from the Mirador del Río

Graciosa, with the smaller islands of Montaña Clara and Alegranza in the distance. The stretch of water separating Graciosa from the mainland is called a *río* (river) but is, in fact, a narrow channel in the Atlantic.

A clifftop stretch of road leads along the Risco de Famara, then to lower ground. The views are wonderful, but don't stop to enjoy them until you find a suitable place, as the road is very narrow. You pass the oddly named village of Yé before reaching **Parque Tropical** (www.guinatepark.com; daily 10am–5pm; charge) at **Guinate**. This is a great family outing, although, at €14 (€6 for children age 4–13), it ought to be.

As well as clearly described subtropical plants and a big cactus garden, there is a vast number of exotic birds (the owners claim 1,300), plus a few monkeys rescued from illegal ownership, and the ever-popular meerkats. Those who object strongly to keeping birds in captivity will, of course, give it a miss, but the conditions are good. There is a large walk-through aviary, and the cages otherwise are huge and well furnished with plants, and appear to offer the birds all the freedom they need – except the freedom to fly away, of course. Parrot shows are held at intervals throughout the day, and there is a café with reasonably priced snacks and light meals.

Meerkats in the Parque Tropical

Haría

Continuing south, you drop down into the greenest, most
fertile part of the island, the valley of **Haría**, known as the
'Valley of a Thousand Palms'. This is an exaggeration, but
there are quite a lot of them. As tour guides and brochures
are keen to point out, the legend recounts that once upon a
time a palm tree was planted for every girl born locally, and
two for every boy. Haría is a nice little town (although a
place of confusing road signs). Spick and span in white and
green, it has attracted a number of artists and artisans in its
time, and became Manrique's home during his later years.
The church, **Nuestra Señora de la Encarnación**, is a modern copy of the 17th-century original which was damaged
by a storm, then destroyed, in the 1950s. There's a good
craft market in the square around the church (Plaza de León
y Castillo) every Saturday. Much of the work on sale is made
at the **Taller de Artesanía** (Tue–Sat 10am–1.30pm, 4–7pm,
Mon 10am–1.30pm; free), a craft-workers' co-operative.

Orzola and Isla Graciosa

At the tip of the island, with its back to the badlands, lies the
village of **Orzola**, jumping-off point for Isla Graciosa.
There's not much to Orzola, apart from a number of good
fish restaurants *(see page 107)*, from the terraces of which
you can watch the comings and goings of boats to the island
(see page 85 for details). The trip to **Isla Graciosa** takes
about 20 minutes, but it leads
you into another world. Part
of the protected **Parque
Natural del Archipélago
Chinijo**, it has only one settlement, Caleta del Sebo,
and a population of 630.
There are no cars, except a

Parking in Orzola

There are car parks just
inland from Orzola harbour;
the bays directly in front of
it only allow you to park
for 2½ hours – no good if
you're going to the island.

Daredevil goat at Las Pardelas

few Land Rovers and, apart from the *paseo* around the harbour, no paved roads. To get around, you have to walk, or hire a bike, which is easily done from a couple of outlets by the port. There are several fish restaurants around the harbour and in the streets behind it, but if you come on a weekday they may not all be open. Most people buy picnic supplies from one of three little supermarkets and head for the beaches. There's a small golden beach and protected waters right by the harbour where local children splash about, but the better beaches are a little way away. The currents are very strong, so swimming is not a good idea. Paddle instead, and explore the rock pools where tiny fish swim around your feet.

If you are back at the harbour around 3pm you'll see the fishing smacks come in, and you can watch as small fish are unloaded from the decks into wheelbarrows and taken a few yards away to be laid out on the jetty to dry in the sun. These are *pejines*; when dried, they are grilled and eaten as tapas.

Back on the mainland, going south from Orzola, the best route is along the coast, but there is a narrow lane out of the village that takes you back to the main Arrieta to Mirador del Río road, and a short way up the lane is **Las Pardelas** (www.pardelas-park.com; daily 10am–6pm; charge). This friendly, family-run ecological park with indigenous plants, domestic animals and donkey rides has a small restaurant, and makes a nice gentle stop if you are travelling with children.

THE CENTRE

The centre of the island is where you will find the airport, the capital, Arrecife, the two largest resorts, Puerto del Carmen and Costa de Teguise, the historic town of Teguise, a number of interesting rural museums, the wine-producing zone and the stunning Fundación César Manrique.

Costa Teguise

Costa Teguise is the only resort north of Arrecife. You enter on the Avenida del Mar (about 14km/8 miles from the airport, 6km/4 miles from the capital), a broad road lined with squat palm trees and flanked by hotels and apartment blocks. The main street, Avenida de las Islas Canarias, parallel to the coast, is lined with commercial centres, small supermarkets, several clinics and a plethora of car-hire outlets.

◀ ⑩

Teguise, the first colonial capital of Lanzarote

Manrique designed the **Pueblo Marinero** at the southern end of the resort, and this is the most appealing part of the development. Low, whitewashed houses with blue or green balconies are clustered in narrow streets around a small square, and it does genuinely resemble a fishing village – which is what Pueblo Marinero means. Later construction, running down to the beach, was taken over by other, less purist hands. A clutch of restaurants and bars here offer fish and chips, hamburgers and pizza, and many have English names – including The Sunburnt Arms. Round the rocky headland there are more buildings going up, and there's a small beach, **Playa del Jablillo**, with a rather unlovely view of the desalination plant just outside Arrecife.

Running northwards, the **Playa de las Cucharas** and **Playa de los Charcos** merge. The former has the better beach, a long stretch of golden imported sand superimposed on the natural volcanic black, and a stretch that is popular with windsurfers, as the winds on this coast are often strong. There is sand on Playa de los Charcos, too, but here are black rocks to clamber over between sand and sea.

A landscaped promenade runs the length of the beaches, with a scattering of cafés and restaurants, and passes the smart Hotel Meliá Salinas, designed by Manrique, which in the 1970s became the first to be built here. The early ambitions for Costa Teguise have not been realised; it lacks a real heart and is more downmarket than the other two major resorts. As a base for exploring the island, however, it has its advantages, as it is very convenient for visiting the cultural sites and villages in the north and centre of Lanzarote.

Fundación César Manrique

From the *circunvalación* around Arrecife the LZ1 leads some 5km (3 miles) to **Tahiche**, where, on the outskirts, you will find the **Fundación César Manrique** (www.cesarmanrique.com; daily 10am–6pm; charge). This was the artist's home, which he remodelled as a museum and gallery when creating the foundation in 1982. All is white: outside, paths and walls gleam like icing sugar on a cake; inside, the marble floors blend with the white walls. Huge windows give views over the surrounding landscape, where the coils of molten lava look as if they might still be liquid. The exhibition salons contain Manrique's own paintings, ceramics and sketches, as well as works by Picasso, Tàpies and Miró. Steps lead down to a series of volcanic bubbles, where trees reach up for the light. A subterranean garden has a pool and retains the atmosphere of a private home, with a huge barbecue and

Manrique's abstract mural at the Fundación

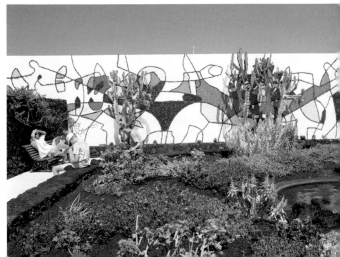

benches built into the walls. As you leave the building you pass through a small garden with a central pond and fountain, and a huge abstract mural that is one of Lanzarote's iconic sights.

Rural Heartland

About 8km (5 miles) west of the foundation you come to the sleepy little town of **San Bartolomé**. The parish church (often closed), the Teatro Municipal and the Ayuntamiento (Town Hall) form two sides of an attractive square with a colonnade, palm trees and a central fountain. Opposite, an open-ended plaza, planted with palms, cacti and oleanders, leads, via broad steps, down to the **Museo Tanit** (Mon–Sat 10am–2pm; charge), an ethnographic museum that outlines the history of the island's earliest inhabitants and has displays on two centuries of island life.

A right turn from the outskirts of San Bartolomé takes you the short distance to **Mozaga** and the **Monumento del Campesino** (Monument to the Countryman), which is set in the exact centre of the island. Manrique's huge white sculpture depicts the *campesino*, surrounded, on the four compass points, by a camel, a donkey, a dog and a goat – although the abstract nature of the construction means that you need a bit of imagination to discern their figures.

Beside the monument a collection of attractive white buildings with green shutters comprise a bar and restaurant (daily noon–4.30pm) and the **Centro de Artesanía** (daily 10am–6pm; free). You can skirt the restaurant to reach the artisans' centre, but don't – if you enter via the huge, domed structure you go through a rocky tunnel and a cool grotto to reach your destination. On the ground floor around a square are workshops where demonstrations of weaving, leather-working and pottery take place. Upstairs a small museum displays models of Lanzarote's early *ermitas* (chapels) and some excellent Naïve ceramic works portraying primitive figures grinding and milling wheat.

The road leads north from the monument towards **Tiagua**. On the far side of the village you reach a tiny white *ermita*, and a right turn leads to the **Museo Agrícola El Patio** (www. museoelpatio.com; Mon–Fri 10am–5.30pm, Sat 10am–2.30pm; charge). A museum of agriculture might not be your first idea of fun, but this one is a delight. On a small estate, once a rural centre where corn was brought to be milled, a fascinating collection of agricultural and domestic objects (complete with some spooky figures, their faces made from gourds) has been gathered. Set in grounds where chicken scratch in the dust and a donkey, goat and camel keep the farmyard theme alive, the museum is housed in a farmhouse dating from 1840 and a large converted barn. Perhaps the most interesting of the displays are numerous old photos,

Remnants of a bygone age in El Patio Museum

dating from the early 20th century to the 1960s, depicting the hardships and the community spirit of rural life. Leaving the museum, you pass through the old bodega, where you will be offered a glass of local wine. A quotation on the museum wall by Tenerife-born writer Agustín Espinosa (1897–1939) reads: 'A land without traditions, without a poetic atmosphere, faces the threat of extinction.' This place is doing all it can to keep those traditions and atmosphere alive.

Teguise

14 **Teguise** was the first colonial capital of the island, built in the centre in the hope that it would be safe from pirate attacks. As you will learn if you visit the Castillo de Santa Bárbara *(see page 48)*, this was not the case, but 'the royal town', as it was known, remained the capital until 1852. It is an attractive place, a village more than a town, with cobbled streets and a number of well-restored colonial buildings with typical Canarian wooden balconies and pretty courtyards.

Sunday is **market day** in Teguise, and tourists from all over the island descend on the little town – coach tours run from all the resorts. If you come by car, a series of car parks on the approach to town make life easy; attendants collect a small fee. The market sprawls all over Teguise, and there's a lively atmosphere, although you won't find much that you couldn't get in tourist shops and markets in any resort in Europe. Even the food on sale in the stalls and kiosks tends towards hamburgers, doughnuts and pizza rather than anything local. There are several good restaurants, though, where you can find Canarian food *(see page 110)*, and a number of shops

Teguise carnival

Teguise has a very lively carnival in February or early March, in which characters dressed as devils and brandishing goatskin truncheons attempt to terrorise carnival revellers.

with more interesting goods: aloe vera products of all kinds are sold in several places, as are local cheeses, wine and jars of *mojo* sauce, a few ceramics and woven goods. There is also an outlet of the Manrique Foundation. Around midday there is a 30-minute exhibition of *lucha canaria (see page 82)* in the village centre, and performances of Canarian music by traditionally dressed local folkloric groups.

The popular market at Teguise

There are three impressive churches in Teguise, two of them monastic, but despite advertised opening hours, you may not find them open. The **Convento de Santo Domingo** (Sun–Fri 10am–3pm, when there is an exhibition), founded by the Dominican Order in 1698, has now become an art centre, which holds regular exhibitions of contemporary work. The church itself is worth a look: it has two naves, and the chapel dedicated to the Virgen del Rosario is the only one in Lanzarote where the retrochoir (the area directly behind the altar) features painted murals.

The **Convento de San Francisco** (Wed–Fri and Mon 10am–4pm, Sat–Sun 11am–3pm; free) founded by Franciscans in the late 16th century, houses a museum of sacred art. If it is closed you will have to be content with admiring the splendid main doorway. The **Iglesia de Nuestra Señora de Guadalupe** is an eclectic mixture of styles, having been

Convento de San Francisco

remodelled many times during its long history, following pirate attacks and fires. Again, you may not find it open, but do not despair – Teguise has some great domestic architecture, especially the **Casa-Museo Palacio Spínola** (Mon–Fri 10am–5pm, Sat–Sun 10am–4pm; charge), which is a delight. Built for an aristocratic family in the mid-18th century, it was restored in the 1970s, purchased by the local authorities and in 1989 became the official residence of the Canary Islands Autonomous Government. A series of beautifully furnished rooms, with wide, polished floorboards, beamed ceilings and lattice-work balconies and cupboards, is ranged around an internal patio, bright with bougainvillea, and an external one shaded by a huge fig tree.

The second of Teguise's palaces, now a small gallery for the works of local artists, is the **Palacio de Herrera y Rojas** (Mon–Sat 10am–1.30pm when there is an exhibition; charge). The third, the **Palacio del Marqués**, is now a restaurant and tapas bar, the Patio del Vino *(see page 110)*, where, for the price of a drink (if you do not want a meal), you can admire the elegant dining room and shady patio.

A final place to visit lies just outside Teguise (take a right turn from the main road and drive up a steep but well-surfaced road). This is the **Castillo de Santa Bárbara y Museo del Emigrante** (Mon–Fri 9am–3pm, Sat–Sun 9.30am–3pm; charge), set on the top of the long-extinct Volcán de Guanapay. Built in the mid-16th century, this imposing building gave refuge to the people of Teguise and the surrounding countryside during repeated attacks by Turkish, French and English pirates. One particularly ferocious attack left the streets of Teguise running with blood – there is a street called the Callejón de la Sangre (Alley of Blood) – the island ransacked and the people starving. The castle is worth a visit to learn about local history and admire the far-reaching views, but the museum, devoted to Canarian emigration from the 16th to the early 20th century, is the most fascinating aspect. Documents, personal effects and early photographs tell the story of a poverty-stricken people who left for the Americas, either seeking a better life or, during a period in the 17th and 18th centuries, sent by the Spanish Crown to populate the colonies.

The Casa-Museo Palacio Spínola in Teguise

Tinajo

From Teguise a road leads 5km (3 miles) northwest to **Tinajo**. The **Iglesia de San Roque** has statues by José Luján Pérez (1756–1815), the renowned Canarian sculptor. However, you must take your chance on finding it open. Nearby, the village of **Mancha Blanca** is best known for the **Ermita de los Dolores**. Inside is a statue of Nuestra Señora de los Volcanes, who is credited with saving the village by halting the lava flow from a volcanic eruption in 1824. Even if the church is closed, the snowy-white exterior is very pretty. The peace of the village is only disturbed on 15 September when a pilgrimage *(romería)* brings people from all over the island, and a craft fair, the Feria Insular de Artesanía Tradicional, is held. From here it's a very short distance to the Timanfaya National Park Visitors' Centre, but this is best saved for a separate visit to the park *(see page 54)*.

The Rocky Coast

Instead, go north to La Santa, a village on the rocky coast that has prospered because of the proximity of the **Club La Santa** (www.clublasanta.co.uk). With facilities for 64 Olympic sports, the club has a vast stadium, an Olympic-sized pool, an artificial lake for windsurfing, and plenty of facilities for people of all abilities (or none), as well as those designed for training serious international sportspeople. If you want to visit the fishing village of **La Caleta de Famara**, the only other settlement on this coast, you must go back to Tiagua (about 12km/8 miles) and take another road north. There are a few good fish restaurants here and an excellent sandy beach, but strong winds make it unsafe for swimming.

Back at the centre of the island (the Monumento del Campesino is an excellent marker), a road runs southwest through **La Geria** wine country. You could stop at the **Bodega El Grifo Museo del Vino** (daily 10.30am–6pm; charge). Set in an old bodega, the museum exhibits wine-making equipment and has a good display on barrel-making; and, of course,

Club La Santa

Vines growing on *picón* soil in La Geria wine country

there's wine for sale. Next door to El Grifo is the **Bodega Barreto**, owned by the oldest wine-producing family on the island. There is no museum here, but you can sample and purchase their wine. Drive on through the landscape of coiled lava and vineyards, where the vines growing in the *picón* (cinders) are planted within semicircles of volcanic rocks to stop the soil blowing away in Lanzarote's strong winds. This road will take you to Uga and the Parque Nacional de Timanfaya *(see page 54)*.

Puerto del Carmen

Lying just 5km (3 miles) west of the airport, **Puerto del** 16 **Carmen** is Lanzarote's biggest resort. Its splendid beaches, Playa Grande and Playa de los Pocillos, and the less popular Playa Matagorda (closest to the airport), extend eastwards for 6km (4 miles) from the little fishing harbour that was the heart of the original village.

Until the 1970s this was just a quiet fishing community, and the area around the pretty harbour retains its village atmosphere. There is a little church here, **Nuestra Señora del Carmen**, but you will only find the doors open for Mass (Sat 8.30pm, Sun 11am and 7pm). There are numerous fish restaurants, too, mostly with excellent views. You can still see fish being unloaded from small fishing smacks by the jetty, but these vessels have been joined by leisure craft and excursion boats offering trips around the coast and across to Fuerteventura. The little rocky coves just east of the harbour, before the beaches begin, are popular with divers.

The golden sands of **Playa Grande**, lined with sunbeds *(hamacas)* and bright umbrellas for rent, offer all kinds of diversions – banana boats, pedalos in the shape of giant swans, beach cafés and, of couse, glorious waters. Parallel to the beach is the **Avenida de las Playas**. Along the sea-side

The inviting sands of Puerto del Carmen

runs an attractive promenade, planted with palms and flowering shrubs. Here you'll find a helpful little **tourist office** (Mon–Fri 9am–1pm, 4.30–7.30pm, Sat 9am–1pm), next door to a small gift shop belonging to the Fundación Manrique, as well as Lanzarote's only **casino**, a couple of nice restaurants, and a few little villa complexes. On the other side, the avenue resembles a vast amusement arcade, lined with cafés, bars and restaurants – mostly with Irish or English names, advertising Guinness, fish and chips and all-day English breakfasts – along with tourist-oriented shops and kiosks offering tattos and hair-braiding. At intervals there are *centros comerciales*, with more shops and restaurants, and it is here that most of the late-night bars and clubs are found. Just past a rocky headland, the Punta de Barranquillo, these commercial outlets peter out, to be replaced with smart little residential complexes. Then, where the **Playa de los Pocillos** commences, so do more shops and bars, but these are far more low-key than the earlier ones.

Puerto Calero is named after the developer José Calero, who initiated the construction of the marina in 1986. It lies about 4km (2½ miles) south of Puerto del Carmen and styles itself a *puerto deportivo* – a sports port. Its smart harbour is full of sleek yachts, its restaurants full of sleek people. You can charter a boat if you fancy a day's deep-sea fishing *(see page 84)*. If you're just dropping in for a look around, it's easiest to take a boat trip from Puerto del Carmen, so you don't have to worry about parking, which can be a problem.

THE SOUTH

The south of Lanzarote encompasses the extraordinary volcanic wilderness of the Parque Nacional de Timanfaya, the pretty, arty village of Yaiza, Playa Blanca with its splendid beaches, and the wild jagged coast to the west.

A camel ride around the volcanic slopes

Parque Nacional de Timanfaya

Going south from the airport, take the LZ2 motorway towards Tías, from where a straight (but non-motorway) stretch continues to Yaiza (about 18km/11 miles). Just before Yaiza lies the little village of **Uga**, looking like a Moorish settlement, with flat-roofed white houses surrounded by palms. About 3km (2 miles) further on a bypass encircles Yaiza. From a roundabout as you approach is a narrow road leading to the **Parque Nacional de Timanfaya** (www. lanzarote.com/timanfaya; daily 9am–5pm; charge). On the way up you pass the **Echadero de Camellos** (Camel Station) where visitors are taken for rides around the outer volcanic slopes on dromedaries. There is also a small museum of volcanic rocks here. The national park is one place that all visitors to Lanzarote include on their itineraries, and it's a place that few will ever forget. It is an experience that makes one aware of the awesome power of nature.

Bus tours around the **Montañas del Fuego** (Mountains of Fire) start from outside El Diablo restaurant and run throughout the day. There is a good recorded commentary in Spanish, English and German, giving background information about the park and about the volcanic eruptions that caused this once fertile area to be turned into a sea of lava. There are frequent photo stops at particularly dramatic points, but you are not allowed to get off the bus. Once the tour is over, most visitors stop for a while to watch park attendants throwing dried brush into a hole in the ground, whereupon flames roar upwards; or pouring buckets of water into a small crater, causing a cascade of boiling water to shoot into the air.

In the glass-sided restaurant, designed, of couse, by César Manrique, you can have a drink or snack, or eat meat that has been grilled over the natural heat emanating from just below the surface (you can watch chefs officiating over the barbecue at the back of the restaurant, so you know that they are not cheating).

Visiting Timanfaya National Park

At the entrance to the park, where Manrique's famous 'fire devil' sign stands, is a barrier, where you pay an entrance fee. You will probably have to join a queue while you wait for a space to become available in the car park, from where buses take visitors on a 40-minute tour of the Ruta de los Volcanes (included in the entrance price). At busy times – late morning seems to be prime time – the wait may be as long as an hour. Take drinking water and something to amuse children when they get bored. You are not allowed to walk, or drive, through the centre of the park, but you can drive around the periphery, and drop in at the Interpretation and Visitors' Centre at the Tinajo end. Any cars you see going straight ahead instead of waiting at the barrier are doing just that.

Yaiza

The visit over, return to the roundabout and take the road
18 straight into **Yaiza**. This village relishes its reputation as the
prettiest on Lanzarote – and it certainly is extremely picturesque. Some typically Canarian-style buildings survived
the eruption that wiped out most of the village in the 1730s,
and these have been complemented by later ones in the same
style. Palms line the road as you approach, scarlet geraniums
decorate green balconies and bougainvillea drips over snowy-
white garden walls.

In the central square is the church of **Nuestra Señora de
los Remedios**, which has columns of volcanic rock and a
beautiful painted wooden ceiling; unlike many of the island
churches, it is usually open. By contrast the **Galería Yaiza**
(Mon–Sat 5–7pm; free), at the west end of the village, has
good exhibitions of contemporary art, but the limited opening hours mean you have to make a special effort to see them.

Yaiza has several nice places to stay and a couple of good
restaurants *(see pages 140 and 111)*. The famous **La Era**,
set in an 18th-century farmhouse converted by Manrique,
reopened under new management in 2011.

Playa Blanca

The road from Yaiza leads south, through the bare, flat lands
19 called El Rubicón, to **Playa Blanca**. This is Lanzarote's third
resort, smaller, quieter and more upmarket than the other
two. It used to be a flourishing fishing village, and retains
something of that atmosphere, even as it has expanded.

The heart of the resort centres on the main street, Avenida de Papagayo, its pedestrianised extension, Calle Limones,
and the Paseo Marítimo, a promenade lined with restaurants
that runs parallel to the soft sands of **Playa Dorada** (Gold-
en Beach) and **Playa Blanca** (White Beach) and leads to the
port. West of the port, another tree-lined promenade runs

One of Playa Blanca's golden beaches

round the Punta Limones headland to pretty little Playa Flamingo, backed by landscaped gardens, and with calm, safe waters. Across a narrow stretch of the Atlantic, the sands of Corralejo, on Fuerteventura, gleam in the sunlight.

Playa Blanca is big on water sports and all kinds of maritime excursions, whether you want to scuba dive, windsurf or simply take a trip in a glass-bottomed submarine *(see pages 83 and 85)*.

How long Playa Blanca will retain its fishing-village atmosphere is hard to say. Already, *urbanizaciones* stretch to the left and right (where most of the big hotels and villa complexes are situated), and on the approach to the village new buildings are going up fast, although there has been a great deal of controversy about the speed and extent of the developments. To the east of town, new roads lead to the **Marina Rubicón**, a swish sports complex, with a 400-berth marina surrounded by apartments, a huge shopping and leisure centre with tennis courts and a pool, plentiful bars and restaurants, and the five-star Hotel Volcán Lanzarote *(see page 139)*. Not everyone was happy about the marina's construction in 2002, but it has become popular with visitors. TUI cruise ships began visiting Playa Blanca in November 2011, which may change the atmosphere of the resort during the winter months when they stop here.

Further east, in a protected area known as **Los Ajaches**, lie Lanzarote's best beaches – **Playa de las Mujeres** and **Playa del Papagayo**. Be cautious about driving along the dirt road that gives access to them: insurance on hired cars does not cover you for 'off-road' driving, and the emergency services will not come and get you if you run into trouble. If you do drive, note that there is a small toll (currently €3). It's easier, and more pleasant, to take the *Princess Yaiza* Taxi Boat (tel: 928 514 322/928 519 012), which leaves four times a day from the harbour and the Marina Rubicón.

Salinas de Janubio and El Golfo

Parallel to the main road from Yaiza is another, the 701, which branches off westwards to the **Salinas de Janubio**. Salt production was one of the most important industries in

Particles of Peridot

The glimmers and glitters you will notice in the black-sand beach at El Golfo come from tiny particles of peridot, a semi-precious stone that is also called olivine, and ranges in colour from olive to lime-green. You will see peridot necklaces and bracelets for sale all over the island. It is the August birthstone and is believed to bring good luck. The stones used to be called evening emeralds, and it is said that the crusaders, who found them around the Red Sea, believed they *were* emeralds and brought them back home to adorn churches.

Lanzarote, but its main purpose was to preserve fish rather than for domestic use, and it is not needed in great quantities now that the catch can be refrigerated. These salt pans are the only ones still in use and they are an impressive sight, laid out like a patchwork quilt, the colour of each pan depending on the relative amount of water and salt it contains.

Part of the crater shell, El Golfo

They are also an excellent spot for birdwatching, especially during the spring and autumn migratory periods.

A short way further up this rocky, deeply eroded coast is a spot known as **Los Hervideros** (The Boiling Pans). You will see coaches in the large car park, for this is a stopping point for tours coming from Timanfaya. It gained its name because the seething sea appears to boil in blowholes and underwater lava caves created by a volcanic tube emerging into the sea. Continue up the coast (where there are plenty of lay-bys to allow drivers to stop and admire the craggy coastline) and you soon arrive at **El Golfo**, a fishing village set between volcanic hills and pounding sea. It's just a collection of pretty cottages and fish restaurants, with outside tables by the sea. To the southern side of the village, the shell of a volcanic crater has been eroded into a jagged, richly coloured cliff. At its foot lie a small black beach and a vivid green **lagoon**, also called El Golfo. Park at the entrance to the village and follow a footpath in order to find it.

From El Golfo the 702 leads back to Yaiza, from where you pick up the main road back towards Arrecife and the airport. Your tour of this diverse island is over.

FUERTEVENTURA

On arriving at the coast of Fuerteventura in 1402, Jean de Béthencourt reputedly exclaimed '¡Que aventura más fuerte!' (What a great adventure!). That's one theory about the origin of the island's name. Others, more prosaically, believe it derives from *viento fuerte* – strong wind. Winds are certainly a feature of the island, and one that draws surfers, windsurfers, kitesurfers and parasailors to its gorgeous sandy beaches: the long stretches in the north, around El Cotillo and at Corralejo, now protected in a Parque Natural; and in the south, the sands stretch from Tarajalejo to Morro Jable and beyond. But there is more to Fuerteventura than beaches: the sleepy little towns in the interior are keepers of the island's history, places where life goes on pretty much as it has for centuries. We begin with the capital, then travel north before visiting the centre and south of the island.

THE NORTH

The north of the island is a diverse area that encompasses the capital, Puerto del Rosario; a number of inland towns and villages, set amid bare conical hills, where you can learn about the agricultural past; and the harbours, dunes and beaches of Corralejo to the east and El Cotillo in the west.

Puerto del Rosario

Puerto del Rosario lies about 7km (4 miles) north of the airport. The town was founded in 1795, called Puerto de Cabras (Goat Port), and became the island capital in 1860 (taking over the role from La Oliva). The name was changed

Fuerteventura's desert landscape

Stone fisherman by the sea

in 1956, but the goat motif is evident in statuary and in a pastoral metallic mural. A small, busy port is used by ferries from Arrecife, container ships and, more recently, cruise liners. Puerto del Rosario is not a tourist-oriented town, but is worth a brief visit. The harbour front has been renovated in recent years and is a pleasant place to walk. Palms offer shade along the inland side, and the sea wall is lined with sinuous benches decorated with coloured tiles. An area designated the Parque de Mayores is a kind of outdoor gym for elderly people, with a variety of exercise machines (well used during the cooler hours) and notices warning of the dangers of over-exertion.

The town is known for its **street sculpture**, which ranges from a huge fountain on a roundabout on the Avenida Marítima, to an abstract metallic clock in the centre of town, to two naked dancing women in a square, and simple statues dotted all over the place – a fisherman stands on the sea wall, while an elderly man sits outside the church.

It was the church, dedicated to the **Virgen del Rosario**, that gave the town its new name. It's a simple grey-and-white building, somewhat neglected, standing in a tree-shaded square opposite the the island government offices. To the side of the square is the **Casa-Museo Unamuno** (Mon–Fri 9am–2pm, Sat 10am–1pm; free), the house (then the Hotel Fuerteventura) where the Basque writer and philosopher Miguel de Unamuno (1864–1936) lived when he was exiled here in

1924, regarded as a thorn in the flesh of Miguel Primo de Rivera's dictatorship. Unamuno's time here was brief, but he quickly came to love the island and to appreciate the kindness shown to him by local people. They later reciprocated by erecting a huge statue of him on the lower flanks of Montaña Quemada (Burnt Mountain), just outside Tindaya. The rooms are furnished as they were in Unamuno's time, with portraits and memorabilia, and quotations from his writing are displayed on the walls.

At the roundabout where roads into Puerto del Rosario meet, stands **Las Rotondas**, a huge commercial centre that adds greatly to the town's previously rather limited shopping opportunities with a range of internationally known stores.

Weaving at La Alcogida

Farms and Windmills

From Puerto del Rosario the FV10 runs northwest towards La Oliva. En route, a left turn is clearly signposted to **Tefia** and the **Ecomuseo La Alcogida** (Tue–Sat 10am–6pm; charge). This ingenious complex, which stretches out on either side of the road, is an abandoned farming settlement that has been restored as a museum, and allows visitors to see how rural life was lived, and what farming methods were used, during the last century. You can watch people demonstrating pulled-thread embroidery, basket-work, leather-work and weaving, and try their home-made aniseed bread.

Just past the museum a road leads off to **Los Molinos** – passing, after a few hundred metres, a beautifully restored windmill, which is visible from La Alcogida. Los Molinos is a pretty little seaside village, with a couple of nice restaurants, about 8km (5 miles) west. The latter part of the road runs along the top of a gulley, the Barranco de los Molinos.

Returning to the main road and going north, you pass, on your left, **Montaña Quemada**, where Unamuno's statue blends with its craggy background; a little further on is the cheese-producing town of Tindaya and **Montaña Tindaya** (397 metres/1,303ft), which the island's indigenous people considered a sacred mountain *(see panel)*.

La Oliva

You soon come to **La Oliva**. This sleepy little town was the seat of the Guanche king, Guixe, and briefly served as the colonial capital of the island in the early 18th century. Today, it's a workaday town, centred on a large church, **Nuestra Señora de Candelaria**, with buttressed walls and a square bell tower of volcanic stone, which makes it look as if it is

Chillida's Dream

In 1992 the Basque sculptor Eduardo Chillida put forward an ambitious proposal to create within Montaña Tindaya a vast open space. Nothing would be visible externally, but within the artist hoped to realise 'a utopia... where those who went inside would be able to see the light of the sun, the moon, to see the sea and the horizon...' The Cabildo Insular supported the plan, but there was a great deal of opposition from environmentalists. Whether or not the project would have gone ahead is unknown, as Chillida died in 2002.

Canarian Art Centre in La Oliva

growing out of the rocky landscape. The interior is quite plain, and the pulpit, decorated with pictures of the four Apostles, is supported on a slim, painted pedestal (€1 in a slot by the door gives five minutes' worth of illumination).

From the side of the Ayuntamiento, opposite the church, a straight, broad road leads to the **Casa de los Coroneles**. This grandiose and much-photographed building, with its many balconied windows, was the seat of the military rulers of the island in the early 18th century. After undergoing extensive restoration, the house was officially reopened by the king and queen of Spain in 2006. It is now a cultural centre where exhibitions and concerts are held.

En route to the colonels' headquarters you pass the **Centro de Arte Canario** (Mon–Sat 10am–5pm, Sun 11am–2pm; charge) in the Casa Mané, a converted colonial house. The collection of works by contemporary Canarian, or Canary Island-based, artists is somewhat eclectic, and the sculpture in the extensive cactus garden even more so, ranging from innovative abstract pieces to leaping dolphins and even some (possibly ironic) gnomes. Don't miss the galleries situated down a flight of steps and through the shop (where there are some good posters and prints for sale), as this is where some of the best work is shown, in large, light rooms.

Villaverde and Lajares

From the centre of La Oliva the FV10 leads towards the northwest coast, but it may be worth taking the slightly longer way round (up the FV101 then turning onto the FV109), because you could then stop at **Villaverde**, where the **Cueva del Llano** (tel: 928 851 400; Tue–Sat 10am–6pm; tours; charge) was first opened to the public in 2006. This *jameo*, or lava tube, was discovered in 1979, and a new species of spider, *Arácnido triglobio*, was found to be living

La Rosita provides a glimpse of traditional rural life

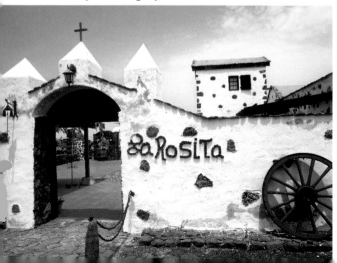

here. A visitors' centre offers information about the *jameo*, which was formed by a lava stream from nearby Montaña Escanfraga. A few kilometres north is **La Rosita** (Mon–Sat 10am–6pm; charge), a farm that demonstrates traditional agricultural methods, including the use of camels on the land. Children especially enjoy contact with the farm animals.

Just before the FV109 joins the FV10 to El Cotillo, you reach **Lajares**, a village with a pair of well-restored wind-mills on the southern outskirts, and a stadium where *lucha canaria (see page 82)* is performed. In the main street is the **Escuela de Artesanía** (Tue–Sat 10am–1pm, 5–8pm, Mon 5–8pm; free). Although called a school, it is really more of a shop, where you can buy handmade products (not cheap) and watch local women embroidering table linen.

El Cotillo

The road continues about 8km (5 miles) to **El Cotillo**. Al- ◀ **6**
though you are greeted, on the outskirts, with a shop pro-claiming that it sells 'best British products', closely followed by a fish-and-chip shop, do not be deterred. This village has a gloriously pretty little fishing harbour and a selection of good fish restaurants to go with it, plus beautiful, windswept dunes and beaches.

Beside the harbour is the **Castillo de Tostón**, a sturdy fortress that houses a tourist information point (Mon–Fri 9am–noon, 1–4pm, Sat–Sun 9am–3pm) and a small gallery (same hours; free) with changing exhibitions of work by local artists. El Cotillo has a small but vibrant artistic communi-ty, with some French connections. From the fort's roof you get wonderful views down the coast. To the north, a narrow road runs through the dunes to the Punta de Tostón, where a lighthouse stands on a headland. A lot of construction work is going on in El Cotillo, and it is to be hoped that the character of the village won't be spoiled.

Corralejo

Return to the main FV101 and after about 6km (4 miles) you
reach **Corralejo**. (You may have started here, having come,
as many do, by boat from Playa Blanca in Lanzarote; *see
page 124*). Corralejo is another tiny fishing village that has
expanded to cope with the demand for tourist accommodation. The heart of the town, the area around the harbour,
still has a character of its own. On **Muelle Chico** (Small
Jetty) there's a **tourist information kiosk** (Mon–Fri
8am–6.30pm, Sat–Sun 8am–3pm) close to a bronze statue
called the **Monumento Marinero**, showing a returned sea-
man embracing his wife and child; nearby, another woman
looks out to sea, waiting for her husband's return. The narrow lanes that radiate from the harbour and the broad main
street, Nuestra Señora del Carmen, filled with cafés, bars and
shops, are reminiscent of an English seaside resort, and not
just because most of the voices you hear are English. There
is also something of a hippy-ish, beachcomber feel here, gen-
erated by the people who come in search of good waves and
a laid-back lifestyle.

In Corralejo you can go diving and scuba diving, take a
beach-buggy trip through the dunes to El Cotillo, hire a
mountain bike, go on a dolphin-watching boat ride or, most
popular of all, take a trip to **Isla de los Lobos** (Island of
Wolves). The wolves in question were the sea lions that flourished here before they were devoured by Norman sailors who
came to the island with Gadifer de la Salle's invasion force
(see page 16). It's a peaceful, pretty place, uninhabited,
although you'll have to share it with lots of other visitors,
and it's small enough to walk around in about three hours.
You can see sea birds – Cory's sheerwaters nest here – and a
variety of vegetation in spring and early summer. The waters
are sheltered and safe even for children to swim, so it is well
worth bringing a picnic and spending a day here.

The Dunes

Drive out of town on the FV1, which runs parallel to the coast through great swathes of **El Jable dunes** that are now protected as the **Parque Natural de Corralejo**. Look out for goats, which sometimes wander in the road – perhaps hoping there is something more interesting than scrubby plants to eat on the other side. On the edge of, but just inside, the park looms the huge Riu Palace Tres Islas Hotel, built before strict planning controls made such construction illegal. Thereafter, there's little but sand and more sand, low brown hills to the right, and a gorgeous sweep of turquoise waters to your left, crashing against the 10km (6 miles) of beach that draw water sports enthusiasts in droves.

The road runs some 35km (22 miles) back to Puerto del Rosario, from where you can begin a tour of the centre and south of the island.

The sweeping expanse of El Jable dunes

Antigua's windmill

THE CENTRE

Visiting the central part of the island offers the contrast of starting out on the coast at Caleta de Fustes, a smart, purpose-built holiday resort, then heading inland to Fuerteventura's first capital, Betancuria, and a number of other pretty towns and villages, set amid stunning mountain scenery and the occasional fertile valley.

Caleta de Fustes

Some 7km (4 miles) south of Puerto del Rosario and 9km (6 miles) south of the airport, on the FV2, lies **Caleta de Fustes**. This is a

completely made-to-measure resort, clustered around a marina and the Castillo de Fustes, the 18th-century fortress from which it takes its name, and spreading inland and along the coast. Opinions are divided on Caleta de Fustes: on the one hand, it has the artificial feel of a resort created from scratch; on the other, it has been well designed, and there's a range of accommodation, good restaurants, and water sports and activities of all kinds, as well as a pleasant sandy beach. The Barceló Club El Castillo, in a prime site right by the beach, is a well-landscaped complex of attractive bungalows that resembles an entire village. To the north, a broad promenade leads along the rocky shore to Costa de Antigua; to the south, construction is going on apace up to and around the garish new Centro Atlántico, opposite which stands Fuerteventura's only McDonald's (so far).

Follow the road a short way south to **Las Salinas** to visit the **Museo de la Sal** (Salt Museum; Tue–Sat 10am–6pm; charge) and the surrounding salt pans, the **Salinas del Carmen**, and learn about the extraction of salt.

Antigua

The road turns inland from here, and after about 10km (6 miles) the FV50 leads off to **Antigua**, set in the very middle of the island. Antigua used to be an important commercial centre and was briefly the capital of Fuerteventura (1834–5). Today it's a quiet town, centred on its sturdy church, **Nuestra Señora de Antigua**, one of the oldest on the island. It stands in a huge paved square, to one side of which a smaller grassy area, the **Plaza de los Caídos**, features a large cross, commemorating those who died in the Civil War. The church has a wooden ceiling and a wide nave, and is largely unadorned apart from a brightly painted main altar.

On the town's northern outskirts is the **Molino de Antigua Centro de Artesanía** (Tue–Sat 10am–6pm; charge). This is a fascinating complex of buildings, set in pleasant gardens, with a collection of cacti. There is a windmill, where you can see the machinery used to grind *gofio*, an archeological museum and an excellent collection of craft work. There is craft work on sale, too, comprising household textiles, woven baskets and hats, and reproductions of Majorero ceramics.

Stop for a view

Just past Antigua the FV416 goes off to the left towards Betancuria. En route, if you want a stunning view over the khaki-coloured landscape and undulating hills, stop at the Mirador Morro Velosa, where there is a well-renovated restaurant and viewing area, designed by César Manrique.

Betancuria

Betancuria is a little jewel of a town, with scarcely a corner that is not picturesque, and it is well aware both of its prettiness and its historical importance. 'Six hundred years of history' announces a sign on the wall of the **Ayuntamiento** (Town Hall) – itself a delightful building with a courtyard you can pop into. This was Fuerteventura's first capital, founded in the early 15th century by Jean de Béthencourt when his original stronghold on the coast proved not strong enough to deter pirate attacks. You can still see the remains of the Franciscan Convento de San Buenaventura, which was established here so that the brothers who followed in the conqueror's wake could bring Christianity to the native people.

There are car parks at either end of the town, which you should use – you cannot drive into the village itself, although there is some roadside parking in the main street. Here you will

Iglesia de Santa María

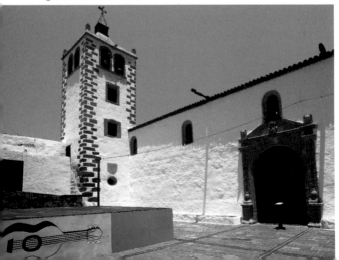

find the **Museo Arqueológico y Etnográfico** (Tue–Sat 10am–6pm; charge), with displays ranging from bones, fossils and some prized fertility idols to Majorero ceramics and information on the first colonisers.

Walk through the cobbled streets to the lovely **Iglesia de Santa María** (Mon–Sat 11am–4pm; small charge), which was consecrated in 1426, destroyed by pirates in 1593 and rebuilt a century later. Entrance to the

Museo de Artesanía

church and the adjoining **Museo de Arte Sacra** usually alternates every half-hour, a rather odd arrangement but one that seems to work.

The church has an intricately carved door, a splendid wooden ceiling and a most unusual floor – large square stones outlined with wooden boards. The ceiling in the sacristy is of Mudéjar design, but decorated with a renaissance painting. There are some real treasures in both the church and the museum, including a lovely retable of La Inmaculada to the left of the high altar and numerous polychromatic wooden figures of saints, some of them salvaged from the convent. The oldest part of the church, the baptistery, has a Gothic ribbed vault.

Across the square from the church, attached to the Casa Santa María restaurant *(see page 113)*, is the **Museo de Artesanía** (Mon–Sat 11am–4pm; charge), arranged around a series of flower-filled courtyards. There are lots of domestic and agricultural implements, women in traditional costume demonstrating weaving, and lots of local produce for sale at very reasonable prices. Sometimes there are wine- and cheese-tastings included. Upstairs, you can watch a short film about the island.

La Vega del Río de las Palmas and Pájara

You drop down now to the 'Valley of Palms', a surprisingly green and fertile region of this dry island, where in mid-September the village of **La Vega del Río de las Palmas** hosts a festival to the Virgen de la Peña (Virgin of Sorrows), patron saint of the island. The rest of the year it's a very sleepy place, but in its main square stands an attractive sandstone **church** (Tue–Sun 11am–1pm, 4–7pm), built in 1666 and dedicated to the Virgin. In the same square, which is lined with Art Deco-style wrought-iron benches, is an excellent restaurant, **Don Antonio** *(see page 113)*.

La Vega del Río de las Palmas

The road twists and turns on its way south, but it is well surfaced, and there's a protective barrier, and lots of lay-bys where you can stop to drink in the splendid views, take photographs, or just let an impatient driver pass you by.

When the road straightens out, you come to the pretty village of **Pájara**. Palms and oleanders line the main street leading to the church

A detail from the doorway of Nuestra Señora de la Regla

of **Nuestra Señora de la Regla** (daily 11am–1pm, 5–7pm), famous for its red sandstone doorway, carved with symbols that apear to be Aztec-influenced, including a figure with a plumed feather headdress. The church has two naves, each with a baroque high altar – put €1 in the box by the door to illuminate them.

Outside the church is a water pump with a long wooden 'arm' to which a camel used to be attached to do the heavy work of pulling up the water. To the side of the church, an attractive park, bright with bougainvillea in summer, lines a dry river bed. Leaving the village to the southeast, you pass a roundabout with a large sandstone statue depicting a farmer milking a goat.

Heading south now, the road rejoins the FV20 which will take you back to the capital or south to the beaches. Even if going south, you could, if you are interested in the island's famous windmills, make a slight detour to **Tiscamanita** where the **Centro de Interpretación Los Molinos** (Tue–Fri and Sun 9.30am–5.30pm; charge) demonstrates the history of milling.

THE SOUTH

It is the beauty of the southern beaches, and the activities they offer, that bring most visitors to Fuerteventura. The combination of barren, elephant-coloured hills, jagged cliffs and great sweeps of white sand is irresistible, and the reliably strong winds promise windsurf enthusiasts the time of their lives. There are also some sheltered coves, though, ideal for those who simply want to enjoy the almost perpetual sunshine. The Sotavento (Leeward) beaches on the east side of the Jandía Peninsula are the most popular; the Barlovento (Windward) beaches on the other side are only for the most hardy and experienced windsurfers. These, and the far tip of the peninsula, Punta de Jandía, are accessible only on tracks that most car-hire companies' insurance will not cover.

Gran Tarajal and Tarajalejo

⑭ **Gran Tarajal**, reached by a straight stretch of road off the FV2, is the island's second-largest port, and therefore has a character of its own that has not been subsumed by the tourist resort that has grown up around it. Narrow streets (where it's very hard to park) lead away from a black-sand beach and a broad promenade, planted with palms and lined with restaurants.

From **Tarajalejo**, a little further down the coast, the main road parallels the shore. Tarajalejo is a fishing village that has developed into a resort but, although it is expanding rapidly, is still low-key and pleasant. It has a 1km (½-mile) pebbly beach and a large main square. The village is popular with sailing enthusiasts and caters well for beginners.

About 5km (3 miles) down the coast, just before the Barranco de Tarajal, lies **La Lajita**, a nice little village with a harbour. On the main road you will find **La Lajita Oasis Park** (daily 9.30am–6pm; charge) with camel rides, giraffes, reptiles, sea lions, parrots and birds of prey, as well as an impressive botanical garden. It's quite expensive, but it makes an enjoyable family day out.

Playas de Sotavento

A little further down the coast a secondary road leads 5km (3 miles) across the narrow neck of the peninsula to the village and beach of **La Pared** (don't ever windsurf here alone – the currents are very dangerous). A wall *(pared)*, built by the Majoreros, stretched across here when the conquerors arrived, and now it roughly forms the boundary of the **Parque Natural de Jandía**, some 14,320 hectares (35,385 acres) in extent, which reaches down to the tip of the peninsula.

Next, you come to **Costa Calma** and the start of the long white beaches of Sotavento. Development at Costa Calma ◀ **15**

One of the idyllic beaches of Costa Calma

began in the 1970s and has expanded ever since, encompassing a variety of accommodation, most of it block-booked by German tour companies, with the hotels providing most of the restaurants and entertainment their guests need.

A little further south, on the beautiful **Playa Barca**, the huge Hotel Meliá Gorriones *(see page 142)* commands a prime position. It is here that the world's largest windsurfing centre, the Pro Center René Egli (www.rene-egli.com), is located, and where the PWA/ISA Windsurfing and the PKRA Kiteboarding World Championships are held in late July–early August. You don't have to be a champion to windsurf here, but you do have to be careful.

Morro del Jable

Continuing down this overdeveloped coast, you will come to **Playa de Matorral** (confusingly also known as Playa de Jandía), where the long white beach has been subject to a rash of huge hotels, apartment blocks, shops and restaurants. A section of the Matorral area has now been designated a Site of Special Scientific Interest, in an attempt to preserve the vegetation and varied bird life of its salt marshes, and an EU project has been launched to raise awareness of the damage that is being done by uncontrolled development. On the **Punta de Matorral** stands a lighthouse, with a little café at its feet.

Playa de Matorral merges

16 ▶ with **Morro del Jable**, the southernmost resort on the peninsula – after this the concrete developments thin out. Morro del Jable is a

Ferry crossings

From Morro del Jable Naviera Armas ferries run to Las Palmas de Gran Canaria seven times a week, taking about 2½–3 hours.

town with a proper port, even though hotels and apartment blocks have stretched their tentacles up the hillsides behind it. There's an attractive seaside promenade, some good fish restaurants and opportunities for all kinds of water sports.

The North of the Peninsula

The roads beyond Morro del Jable down to Puerto de la Cruz and the Punta de Jandía, and round to Cofete on the northern side of the peninsula, are not to be recommended unless you have a four-wheel-drive vehicle, and even then you should check the details of your insurance cover. There is no road going across the peninsula, just a ridge of mountains cut through with *barrancos* (gullies) and dominated by **Montaña de Jandía**, the highest peak on the island at 807 metres (2,648ft). The most common form of vegetation here is the *cardón de Jandía*, the symbol of Fuerteventura.

The beaches at the peninsula's tip and the **Playa de Cofete** and **Playa de Barlovento** (both favoured by nudists) on the other side are largely deserted, undeniably beautiful, and swept by high winds. Rocks are sculpted into jagged forms, sea spurge survives on the dunes, and a few goats are the only sign of wildlife. The tiny hamlet of Cofete is known only for the Villa Winter, an abandoned house built by a Nazi sympathiser on land allegedly given to him by General Franco. All kinds of rumours have surrounded this villa over the years, but this untamed region is just the sort of place in which rumours flourish and myths are created.

WHAT TO DO

Most of the things you can do in Lanzarote and Fuerteventura are done outdoors, many of them on or in the water. Ideal winds and waves make windsurfing the most popular activity, but there are many others – sailing, diving, fishing, swimming and lots of boat trips. On land, there are some good hiking trails, opportunities for horse riding and exploring the rougher terrain by jeep, buggy or quad bike safari, and plenty of activities for children.

SPORTS AND OUTDOOR ACTIVITIES

Windsurfing

On **Lanzarote** the Windsurfing Club Las Cucharas, Centro Comercial las Maretas, Calle Marajo, Costa Teguise, tel: 928 590 731, www.lanzarotewindsurf.com, offers advanced, beginners' and children's courses, plus other activities *(see page 88)*. Windsurf Paradise, Calle la Corvina 8, Playa de las Cucharas, Costa Teguise, tel: 928 346 022, www.windsurf lanzarote.com, also offers lessons, from basic to advanced levels, and surfing trips to other beaches on the island.

On **Fuerteventura** a selection of operators includes: Escuela de Windsurf El Castillo, Caleta de Fustes, tel: 928 163 100; Ventura Surf Center, Avenida Marítima 42, Correlejo, tel: 928 866 295, www.ventura-surf.com; and *the* name in windsurfing, Pro Center René Egli I, Hotel Meliá Gorriones, Playa la Barca, tel: 928 547 483, www.rene-egli.com. There's a second centre, René Egli II, 3km (2 miles) further south, where winds are less strong and there is an area of shallow water more suitable for beginners.

Windsurfing is popular on both islands

Kitesurfing

In **Fuerteventura** try the Fuerteventura Kiteboarding School, El Cotillo, tel: 928 538 504, www.ksfuerte.com, and Flag Beach Windsurf and Kitesurf Centre, tel: 928 866 389, mobile: 609 029 804, www.flagbeach.com, in Corralejo.

Surfing

Lanzarote surf schools include Calima Surf, Caleta de Famara, tel: 626 913 369, www.calimasurf.com; Famara Surf, Avda El Marinero 39, Caleta de Famara, tel: 696 241 952, www.famarasurf.com, for classes at all levels plus equipment; the Quiksilver Surf School, tel: 928 867 307, www.quiksilver-surfschool.com, for surfing (with or without accommodation) in Lanzarote and Fuerteventura; and Windsurf Paradise (see page 81 for details).

There is less surfing in **Fuerteventura**, but Ineika Funcenter, Corralejo, tel: 928 535 744, www.ineika.com, caters

Lucha Canaria

Lucha canaria is a popular sport that dates back to pre-Hispanic times. It is a form of wrestling in which members of two teams of 12 wrestlers take it in turns to throw an opponent to the ground. The bout *(brega)* is lost if any part of a wrestler's body (except his feet, of course) touches the ground. You are most likely to see the sport at village fiestas, and there is usually a demonstration in Teguise on Sunday market day, around noon. It also takes up hours of Saturday-night prime-time television on the regional channel, and generates strong feelings. Another traditional local sport is *juego del palo*, or stick-fighting. The object is to keep the body as still as possible, while fending off the blows from an opponent's stave – a stick about 1.8 metres (6ft) long. Again, you are most likely to see one of these bouts at a village festival; ask at a local tourist office.

for beginners and advanced surfers, and arranges transfers to the best surf spots.

Diving

For diving in **Lanzarote**'s three main resorts, contact Calipso Diving, Pueblo Marinero, Costa Teguise, tel: 928 590 879, www.calipso-diving.com, which runs PADI/BSAC courses, plus family snorkelling excursions; Big

Snorkelling in clear waters

Blue Sea Dive Center, Hotel Galeón Playa, Costa Teguise, tel: 928 346 803, www.lanzarotedive.de, for beginners' PADI courses and advanced courses, children's courses, scuba diving and wreck and cave diving; Manta Diving, Avenida Juan Carlos I 6, Local 5, Puerto del Carmen, tel: 928 516 815, mobile: 649 121 142, www.manta-diving-lanzarote.com, which offers PADI courses and daily dives, and specialises in 'Discover Scuba' shallow-water dives and snorkelling for children. In Playa Blanca the Rubicón Diving Center, Marina Rubicón, tel: 928 349 346, www.rubicondiving.com, runs courses at various levels. On Isla Graciosa dive courses are run at the Archipélago Chinijo Dive Centre (tel: 902 401 666, www.lineasromero.com).

Diving opportunities are numerous on **Fuerteventura**, especially in Corralejo. Abyss Divers, Pro Centre, Calle Gravina 8, Corralejo, tel: 638 722 297 (mobile), www.abyss-fuerteventura.com, is Irish-owned and has a good reputation. Dive Center Corralejo, Nuestra Señora del Pino 22, Corralejo, tel: 928 535 906, mobile: 610 708 344 or 345, www.divecentercorralejo.com, takes divers to more than 40 sites, runs classes at all levels and has an indoor instruction pool. Punta Amanay Dive Center, Calle El Pulpo s/n, Edificio Dunas Club, Corralejo, tel: 928 535 357, mobile: 639 171 949, www.punta-amanay. com, runs dives in El Cotillo, El Jablito, Caleta de Fuestes and Morro Jable, although based in Corralejo. In the south there is Jandia Sub at Sunrise Beach Club Paraíso Playa, Playa Esquinzo, tel: 646 047 282, www. jandiasub.com.

Sport Fishing

The biggest operator in **Lanzarote** runs *Katfish*, *Margarita Segunda*, *Folixa*, and

Fishing can be social or solitary

Ana Segunda from Puerto del Carmen and Puerto Calero marina (tel: 928 514 322, mobile: 629 731 29, www.sportfishinglanzarote.com), offering shark fishing, game fishing, bottom fishing and trawling on well-equipped boats. Transport to and from your hotel and lunch are included in all-day trips. It also does private charters. On **Fuerteventura**, there is fly fishing and angling from *Barvik* on Corralejo's Muelle Deportivo, tel: 928 535 710, and *Pez Velero*, tel: 928 866 173.

Sailing

In **Lanzarote**, Active Adventures (UK tel: 0871 231 1123, www.activeadventures.co.uk), based in Costa Teguise, offers sailing among its many other water-based activities. The Cat

Company (http://catcompany.eu) offers catamaran sailing at various levels, as well as wind- and kitesurfing, on Top Cat catamarans in Tarajalejo and Las Playitas, **Fuerteventura**.

Boat Trips

Among many companies competing for business in **Lanzarote** are Líneas Marítimas Romero, Calle García Escámez 11, Isla Graciosa, tel: 902 401 666/928 842 055, www.lineas-romero.com, with trips from Orzola to Isla Graciosa five times a day in high summer.

Princesa Ico is a glass-bottomed catamaran that makes four trips a day (excluding Thursday and Sunday) between Puerto del Carmen and Corralejo, with dolphin-spotting en route (tel: 928 516 113, mobile: 629 731 293). *Princess Yaiza*, Playa Blanca, is a glass-bottomed boat that runs from Playa Blanca harbour and Marina Rubicón to Playa de Papagayo four times a day (tel: 928 514 322). Note that the boat can't go right to the beach so the last bit is done on a dinghy. Many boat trips can be pre-booked online at www.aquaticket.com, and most companies will pick you up from or near your hotel.

Rubicat, Marina Rubicón, Playa Blanca (tel: 928 519 088, www.marinarubicon. com), a 23m (75ft) catamaran, makes trips to Playa Papagayo, with opportunities for jet-skiing and snorkelling. Submarine Safaris (Módulo C, Puerto Calero, tel: 928 512 898, www.submarine safaris.com), makes trips beneath the sea in a yellow (naturally) submarine.

The yellow submarine

Kicking up dust on a jeep safari

Most of **Fuerteventura**'s boat trips tend to be in the north of the island, where the winds and waves are not as strong as in the south. Catlanza (Puerto de Corralejo, tel: 928 513 022, mobile: 647 061 991, www.catlanza.com) organises catamaran trips to Lanzarote's Papagayo beaches, and also does corporate and private charters. Excursiones Marítimas (Corralejo, tel: 699 687 294, www.excursionesmaritimaslobos.com) run several no-frills trips a day to the Isla de los Lobos on *El Majorero, Isla de Lobos* and *Celia Cruz;* buy tickets at the harbour kiosks. In the south, Subcat (Avda de Saladar 1, Jandía, tel: 900 507 006, www.subcat-fuerteventura.com) takes you 30m (100ft) below the surface.

Jeep and Quad Bike Safaris
In **Lanzarote** there are various jeep and quad bike safaris organised by Biosphere Excursions, Costa Teguise, tel: 928 590 304, MegaFun Lanzarote, Puerto del Carmen, tel: 928

512 893, who run three-hour quad bike excursions, and Jeep Safari Tamarán, tel: 928 512 475, www.lanzarote-tour.com, in Puerto del Carmen, who offer extensive tours of the island from Tahiche to Playa Blanca and will arrange pick ups.

In **Fuerteventura** Discovery Safari, tel: 928 775 188, http://discoverysafari.es, runs jeep tours all over the island, including one that goes across the Jandia peninsula to the deserted Playa Cofete. Fuerte Trike, tel: 928 545 067, www.fuerte-trike.com, organises quad bike tours from various starting points.

Bike Hire and Tours

Road and mountain bikes are available for hire in all the resorts. On **Lanzarote** try Bike Station, Centro Comercial Las Maretas, Avda Isla de las Canarias, Costa Teguise, tel: 628 102 177, www.mylanzarote.com; in Playa Blanca go to Electro Bike, Centro Comercial Punta Limones, tel: 652 200 570, www.electrobike-lanzarote.com; in Puerto del Carmen there's Renner Bike, Avda de las Playas, Centro Comercial Marítimo 25, tel: 928 510 612, www.mountainbike-lanzarote.com.

Fuerteventura has Easy Riders, Calle Las Dunas s/n, Corralejo, tel: 637 408 233, www.easyriders-bikecenter.com, for mountain- and road-bike tours of the north of the island; Backtrax at Hotel Elba Castillo, Caleta de Fustes, tel: 656 753 055, www.backtrax1.com, does off-road motor-bike tours; Caleta Cycles in Caleta de Fustes, tel: 676 600 190 rents bikes and organises tours at various levels; and Ventura Biking, Calle Gran Canaria 2, Corralejo, mobile: 637 408 233, offers mountain-bike tours.

Be prepared

Bike and buggy hire and excursions include insurance (check whether it is third-party or comprehensive) and provide helmets, but you must bring your driving licence and a credit card to acts as as a deposit.

Hiking

On **Lanzarote** Canary Trekking, Calle La Laguna 8, Costa Teguise, mobile: 609 537 684 or 696 900 929, www.canarytrekking.com, conducts guided walks in Timanfaya National Park, the Playa de Famara Natural Park, and the protected landscape of La Geria. Windsurfing Club Las Cucharas *(see page 81)* also offers guided walks through volcanic landscapes. On **Fuerteventura** Caminata, Villa Volcana, Villaverde, tel: 928 535 010, organises a variety of treks on a network of hiking trails.

Horse and Camel Riding

Lanzarote a Caballo, Carretera Arrecife–Yaiza, Km 17, Yaiza, tel: 928 830 038, www.lanzaroteacaballo.com (daily 10am–6pm) offers treks of varying lengths for beginners and experienced riders. Camel rides are also available.

Taking to the saddle at Lanzarote a Caballo

Golf

On **Lanzarote** Costa Teguise Golf Club, Avda del Golf s/n, Costa Teguise, tel: 928 590 512, www.lanzarote-golf.com, is an 18-hole course open to non-members that also offers lessons. On **Fuerteventura** there's the Fuerteventura Golf Resort, Carretera de Jandía, Km 11, Caleta de Fustes, tel: 928 160 005, www.fuerteventuragolfresort.com.

CHILDREN'S ACTIVITIES

There's lots for children to do on both islands, as well as play on the beach. Taking them out in the evening isn't a problem, either, as most restaurants welcome children. Many hotel complexes have entertainment geared to children between three and 10 years old. Most children, except the very young, will also enjoy the boat and submarine trips listed above and many of the activities detailed in the *Where to Go* chapter, such as the bus tour around the Ruta de Volcanos.

Water Parks

There is one on each island. On **Lanzarote** it is Aquapark, Avenida de Teguise, Costa Teguise, tel: 928 592 128, with all the usual pools, chutes, slides and activities (daily 10am–6pm). On **Fuerteventura** there is Baku Park, Corralejo, tel: 928 867 227, www.bakufuerteventura.com (mid-June–mid-Sept daily 10am–6pm; mid-Sept–Nov, Mar–May Mon–Tue, Fri–Sun 10am–5pm), for all kinds of watery fun.

Go-Karting

Go-Karting Club, Carretera Arrecife–Tias Km 7 (2km/1 mile from **Lanzarote** airport), tel: 928 524 956, www.gran karting.com (daily June–Sept 11am–10pm, Oct–May 10am–9pm), offers karts and tracks for children and adults, and even 'mini motos' for the under-fives.

Animal Attractions

One of **Lanzarote**'s best-known attractions is Echadero de Camellos, Parque Nacional de Timanfaya (daily 9am–5pm), where children and adults alike find it hard to resist the camel rides. Lanzarote a Caballo *(see page 88)* is a good riding school for adults and children; they also do paintball sessions. Las Pardelas, Orzola, tel: 928 842 545, www.pardelas-park.com (daily 10am–6pm) is a family-run place with donkey rides and a playground. At Parque Tropical, Guinate (5km/3 miles north of Haría), tel: 928 835 500, www.guinatepark.com (daily 10am–5pm), exotic birds, monkeys and meerkats are the highlights for children. Rancho Texas, Puerto del Carmen, tel: 928 841 286, www.ranchotexaslanzarote.com, puts on several shows a day; there are crocodiles, parrots and birds of prey, canoes and pony rides (daily 9.30am–5.30pm; free transport from resort hotels).

The reptile show at Fuerteventura's La Lajita Oasis Park

One of **Fuerteventura**'s big draws is Oceanarium Explorer, Puerto Castillo Yacht Harbour, Caleta de Fustes, tel: 928 163 514, with a glass-bottomed, non-diving submarine and a catamaran for dolphin-spotting trips. Also popular is La Lajita Oasis Park, Carretera General de Jandía, La Lajita, tel: 902 400 434, www.lajitaoasispark.com (daily 9.30am–6pm), with camel rides, giraffes, reptiles, sea lions, parrots and birds of prey. At Zoo Safari, Carretera Majanicho, Lajares, tel: 928 868 006, there are camel safaris and a chance to explore the crater of Calderón Hondo (daily departures at noon), as well as shorter camel rides closer to the litttle camel farm.

SHOPPING

Shopping is not a major activity on either island, but there are some interesting items. Among them are consumables: *mojo* sauce can be bought in small jars in many places, as can cactus honey, wine from La Geria and the ubiquitous rum-and-honey liqueur called Ronmiel. Majorero cheese, made in Fuerteventura, can also be bought on both islands.

Aloe vera products of all kinds can be found everywhere. There are some specialist shops and stalls in markets, but products are also available in souvenir shops and supermarkets. Lanzaloe is an ecologically aware organisation based in Orzola that supplies large quantities of aloe vera to pharmaceutical and cosmetics companies. Other items include ceramics – nothing startlingly original, but you can find some good modern copies of traditional pottery – and peridot jewellery *(see page 58)*. There is also hand-embroidered table linen and basketwork. The genuine articles are usually found in artisans' centres or museums; because it is such labour-intensive work, they are quite expensive.

Some places in **Lanzarote** worth checking out for comestibles are: Ahumaderia Uga, Ctra Arrecife–Yaiza, Uga, for excellent smoked salmon; El Gourmet Deli, Calle Canalejas 8, Arrecife, which has a good selection of delicatessen items – cheese, ham, *mojo* sauces and honey as well as local wine; and the Bodega El Grifo and Bodega Barreto, next door to each other on the main road at La Florida, which both sell their own wine. The white *malvasía* is best, whether you like it sweet, dry or medium. You can taste before you buy.

For craft work, there is the Taller de Artesanía, Plaza de León y Castillo, Haría, a co-operative that sells pottery, basket work and embroidered items, which can also be found in Haría's Saturday market. A the Centro de Artesanía at the Monumento del Campesino, Mozaga, you can buy traditional-style items made on the premises, as well as wine from nearby La Geria.

Traditional-style ceramics

The Fundación César Manrique in Tahiche has a good selection of items with the artist's designs, ranging from prints and ceramics to canvas bags, scarves and aprons – all very well-priced. The Fundación also has outlets in Teguise and in Puerto del Carmen (next to the tourist office).

Teguise market is the best-known and biggest on Lanzarote, but most of the goods are not local – a lot of them are made in the Far East. However, there are a number of shops in the town that are open on Sunday and sell better-quality stuff. These include: Casa Kaos, Calle León y Castillo, with a good selection of jewellery and pottery, and Galeria La Villa, Plaza Clavijo, a collection of shops selling ceramics, bags and scarves, plus a 'wellness centre' and massage services. The litle complex also contains a small bookshop, Leo-Libros, with books about Lanzarote and the rest of the Canary Islands. Herbolaria Demeter, Calle León y Castillo, specialises in aloe vera products, health food and candles.

Teguise's market

In **Fuerteventura** Majorero cheese is one of the best buys. Hijos de Vera Montelongo, Calle de la Casa Alta 15, Tindaya, is one of the island's best-known cheese makers, and sells direct from its production centre, and from La Casa de Ganadero, Calle Salamanca 12, Puerto del Rosario, which also sells other island produce.

Craft work on Fuerteventura can be found in the Casa Santa María Centro de Artesanía, Betancuria. Traditional woven and embroidered items and pottery are sold in the museum shop, along with *mojo* sauce, cactus honey, wine and liqueurs. At the Escuela de Artesanía Canaria, Plaza Santa María, Lajares, you can see women embroidering table linen by hand, and buy the products.

The best range of contemporary posters, prints and ceramics (along with those at the Fundación César Manrique) can be found at the Centro de Arte Canario, Casa Mane, La Oliva, and they are very reasonably priced.

NIGHTLIFE AND FESTIVALS

Most of the the islands' nightlife is provided either in the resort hotels, which usually have middle-of-the-road live acts
several times a week, or in the bars and discos of the commercial centres, which tend to have quite a high turnover
rate. Temporary structures are often set up on or near the
beaches for performances by rock and pop groups. Corralejo and El Cotillo, on Fuerteventura, have the best reputation
for rock, pop and jazz – posters and flyers in the resorts will
tell you what's on where. Corralejo's best-known live music
venue is the Rock Island Bar, www.rockislandbar.com. El Almacén, Calle Betancort, Arrecife, often has jazz, rock or gui-
tar music on Friday nights (the Cabildo puts out a monthly
leaflet, called *Cultura*, listing events here and in the theatres
in San Bartolomé and Teguise). The centre also has a small
cinema which shows art-house films, but these are all in
Spanish, as are those in Arrecife's mainstream cinema (Multicines Atlántida, Charco de San Ginés).

In October, the Visual Music Festival of Lanzarote stages
performances of contemporary music in interesting venues
all over the island – chiefly
the auditoriums in the Cueva
de los Verdes and the Jameos
del Agua, as well as the
Convento de Santo Domin-
go in Teguise.

There is one casino, Gran
Casino de Lanzarote, Avenida de las Playas 12, Puerto
del Carmen, tel: 928 515
000 (daily 7pm–4am; restaurant 8pm–2am; dress smart-
ly and take your passport).

Making music in Corralejo

Calendar of Events

6 January Cabalgata de Reyes (Procession of the Three Kings), Arrecife. The kings parade through the streets on camels, throwing sweets to children. Some processions in other towns on both islands.

February–early March Carnival. Celebrations, held in most towns and resorts on both islands, staggered so they do not clash with each other. Several days of flamboyant fun start with the *murgas*, a parade of costumed revellers accompanied by whistles and drums. Carnival ends with the *entierro de la sardina*, a strange ritual common to all Spanish carnival celebrations, in which a papier-mâché model of a sardine is burnt.

Late March–mid-April Semana Santa. The week preceeding Easter is a time of solemn processions.

Mid-June Corpus Christi. Intricately designed carpets of salt, dyed various colours, cover the roads around the Iglesia de San Ginés in Arrecife, where processions are held.

23 June San Juan. On the eve of the saint's day bonfires are lit in some town and village squares. The biggest celebration is in Haría.

14 July San Buenaventura. The island's patron saint is celebrated throughout Fuerteventura but especially in Betancuria.

16 July Nuestra Señora del Carmen. The patron saint of fishermen and sailors is celebrated in most coastal places with street processions and decorated boats. Biggest celebrations on Lanzarote are in Puerto del Carmen, Playa Blanca, Isla Graciosa and, although it is inland, Teguise. On Fuerteventura, Morro Jable and Corralejo stage the most colourful events.

25 August San Ginés celebrations, in honour of Arrecife's patron saint include processions and dancing, and last about a week.

Early September Nuestra Señora de los Volcanes. According to legend, the Virgin halted the flow of lava from a volcanic eruption in 1824 and saved the village of Mancha Blanca, Lanzarote. She is honoured with a pilgrimage, a folklore festival, an artisans' fair and bouts of *lucha canaria*. Gran Tarajal, Fuerteventura: Open International Fishing Competition.

Mid-November Kite Festival: Playa del Burro, Corralejo. Kite-flyers from all over the world come to this two-day event.

EATING OUT

Canary Islands food has much in common with that of mainland Spain, but with interesting regional differences. There are also dishes similar to those found in parts of Latin America – although whether these recipes were introduced to the New World by Canarian emigrants, or American inventions brought back by returnees, is debatable.

You will also find some restaurants where the cooking is described as *cocina vasca* (Basque), because a number of cooks from this northern region of Spain have come to work on the island or opened their own restaurants here. Their familiarity with Atlantic fish and seafood may help them feel at home. As the Basque region has a reputation for some of the best cooking in Spain, they are a welcome addition.

Where and When to Eat

When it comes to places to eat, the choices are between the fish restaurants that line the seafronts and harbours; the places serving typically Canarian food, which are found mainly in the towns and villages – although there are a few in the resorts; and the all-purpose pizza, pasta and burger joints. There are a few expensive venues, but most are very reasonably priced. You may see restaurants advertising *cocina casalinga* or *comidas caseras* – this simply means home cooking, and, while the quality may vary, it is a sign

Authentic offerings

In the resorts, you may have to bypass numerous restaurants offering burgers, chips, pasta and pizza, not to mention all-day English breakfasts, before you find ones serving genuinely Canarian – or even Spanish – food, but they do exist. And good fresh fish, simply cooked, can be found almost everywhere.

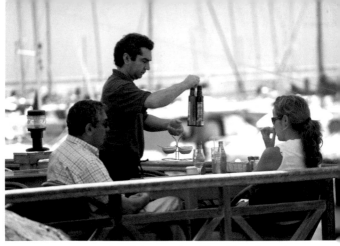

Lunch is served on Playa Blanca's marina

that you will be getting authentic, and inexpensive, island food. There are not many places that style themselves tapas bars, but in many middle-of-the-range and inexpensive restaurants there will be a variety of tapas on offer, and some of the portions are quite large – two or three would make a meal for most people. You will also see *raciones* (portions) advertised: these are larger than tapas, but not full meals.

Bars are generally places in which to drink, not eat, although many will serve sandwiches *(bocadillos)* or a limited range of tapas. A *piscolabis* is a bar serving a variety of little sandwiches and snacks. *(See pages 106–14 for a selection of recommended restaurants.)*

The islanders, like the people of mainland Spain, eat late. Between two and three o'clock is the time to sit down to lunch, and ten o'clock is not too late for dinner. Some restaurants may close between lunch and dinner, but many serve food all day. Those that cater mostly to foreign visitors, aware that habits are different, will have their lunch menus out by midday and serve dinner as early as you like.

Sunday lunch is a major event, and as this continues throughout the afternoon many restaurants are closed on Sunday evening. Some also close one evening during the week, and a number of places will close for a month in early summer to prepare themselves for their busy season in July and August.

Fish

The waters around the islands are rich in fish, which turn up on menus in the restaurants. Along with the ubiquitous *sardinas*, fresh from the ocean, the fish most commonly seen on menus are *corvina* (a kind of sea bass), *cherne* (wreck-fish or stone bass), *sama* (sea bream) and *bacalao* (salt cod). You will also find *merluza* (hake), *atún* (tuna) and seafood such as *gambas* (prawns), *pulpo* (octopus), *calamares*

Cheese

Fuerteventura is known for its goat's cheese, Majorero, which has been awarded a *denominación de origen controlada* (DOC) and is said to be one of the best of its kind in Spain. Goat's milk – which must be unpasteurised to make the cheese – has a high fat content and is very aromatic. The young, fresh cheese has a white rind and a crumbly texture; the matured version has a yellow rind, which may be rubbed with oil or paprika or, sometimes, *gofio*. You will find it on most menus in Fuerteventura, and quite a few on Lanzarote. You will also see cheeses from Gran Canaria: *queso de flor*, a soft cheese that is a mixture of sheep's and cow's milk curdled with the juice of flowers from the cardoon thistle; and *queso tierno de Valsequillo*, which ranges in flavour from mild to strong – the stronger it is the darker the colour.

(squid) and *almejas* (clams).

Fish will often be served simply grilled along with salad, *mojo* sauce and *papas arrugadas (see page 100)*, but there are numerous other ways that it may appear on your table. *Sancocho canario* is a popular dish, a stew made with red grouper or sea bass, potatoes and yams, spiced up with a hot variety of *mojo*

Fresh grilled fish

sauce. *Salpicón de pescado* is another dish you may see on menus; this is sea bass cooked, chopped and served cold with a mixture of onions, garlic, tomatoes and peppers, topped with hard boiled egg and olives. A delicacy introduced from the Basque country is *calamares rellenos de bacalao* – small squid with a cod-based stuffing, sometimes served in a creamy sauce (a similar dish is made with stuffed peppers – *pimientos*).

Paella is not a Canary Island dish, but you can still find it, along with other rice and seafood dishes such as *arroz negra* (rice with squid and squid ink, which makes it black).

Meat

If you don't like fish, don't despair – there's plenty of meat to be found. *Cabrito* (kid) and *conejo* (rabbit) are most common, but pork *(cerdo)* and chicken *(pollo)* are popular, and there are some good steaks to be had as well. Goat and rabbit are often served *al salmorejo* (with green peppers, in a herb and garlic marinade). Chorizo – the red spicy sausage found all over Spain – also crops up in a variety of guises.

Soups

Most of the world's traditional dishes originated as a way of filling stomachs with what was available and inexpensive. In the Canary Islands, this meant a whole range of substantial soups and stews. *Ropa vieja* (literally, old clothes) may not sound very appetising, but it's a tasty mixture of meat, tomatoes and chickpeas; *puchero* includes meat, pumpkin and any vegetables available; while *rancho canario*, made with chicken, chorizo, bacon, chickpeas and various herbs, is the most elaborate and, some say, the best.

Vegetarians should be aware that even such innocent-sounding dishes as watercress soup *(potaje de berros)*, a staple found on many menus, has chunks of bacon in it, and celery soup *(potaje de apio)* may contain scraps of pork.

Vegetables

The vegetables you are offered will be those that are in season, and, because the island does not produce a great variety and imports are expensive, choice may be limited. Pulses such as lentils *(lentejas)* and chickpeas *(garbanzos)* are used a lot. Canary tomatoes are delicious – although most of those you get here will have been imported from Gran Canaria – and Lanzarote onions are far sweeter than those from mainland Spain. If you like garlic, ask for *tomates aliñados*, tomato salad smothered with olive oil and garlic. *Pimientos de padrón* – small green peppers cooked whole and covered with salt – originated in Galicia and are now found everywhere. Avocados (strictly speaking a fruit, not a vegetable) are served at a perfect stage of ripeness.

Most dishes contain or are accompanied by potatoes *(papas)*. You won't go far without encountering *papas arrugadas* (wrinkled potatoes), which are served with meat and fish or by themselves as tapas. They are small potatoes – the yellow-fleshed Tenerife variety are best – cooked in their skins in salted water, then left to dry over a low heat until their skins wrinkle and a salty crust forms. It is said that this dish originated with fishermen, who used to boil the potatoes in sea water.

Mojo

Papas arrugadas, and many meat dishes, are usually accompanied by *mojo rojo*, a sauce whose basic ingredients are tomatoes, peppers and paprika. A spicier version *(mojo picón)* contains hot chilli pepper as well. *Mojo verde* is a green sauce made with oil, vinegar, garlic, coriander and/or parsley, usually served with fish. The sauces arrive at the table in small bowls, so you can use as much or as little as you like. Every restaurant – and probably every home – seems to have their own version, and entire *mojo* recipe books are published.

Mojo rojo and mojo verde

Gofio

Made of wheat, barley or a mixture of the two, *gofio* was the staple food of the Guanches and still forms an essential part of the diet today. The cereal is toasted before being ground into flour, and then has a multiplicity of uses. It is stirred into soups and into children's milk, used to thicken sauces, and mixed with oil, salt and sugar into a kind of bread, not unlike polenta. It is also blended with fish stock to make a thick soup called *gofio escaldado*.

Fruit and Desserts

There is not enough rain to grow much fruit in Lanzarote or Fuerteventura, but products imported from mainland Spain or the other islands are usually delicious when in season. On many menus desserts are limited to ice cream *(helado)*, flan (the ubiquitous caramel custard), fresh fruit, dried fruit and nuts, and the one you see everywhere, *bienmesabe*, which translates as 'tastes good to me' – and so it does. There are numerous recipes, but basically it is a mixture of crushed almonds, lemon, sugar (lots), cinnamon and egg yolks.

Dried fruit and nuts are often found on the dessert menu

What to Drink

The breakfast drink is coffee. *Café solo* is a small, strong black, like an espresso; a *cortado*, served in a glass, is a shot of coffee with a small amount of hot milk; *café con leche* is a large milky coffee. An *Americano* is a shot of coffee with added hot water. However, espresso and cappuccino are widely understood terms.

At bodegas you can try wine from the barrel before buying

Hot chocolate is sometimes available for breakfast, but if you ask for tea you will just get a teabag in a little pot.

You are advised not to drink tap water, but *agua mineral* is available everywhere – *con gas* is sparkling, *sin gas* is still. *Zumo de naranja*, freshly squeezed orange juice, is widely available, and in some bars you can get more exotic juices.

Wine is usually drunk with meals, most of it imported from the mainland; Rioja is one of the favourites. But Lanzarote does produce its own wine: *malvasía*, known in English as malmsey. Shakespeare alluded to malmsey several times, and the duke of Clarence drowned in a vat of it in 1478. Although this is best known as a sweet wine, there are excellent dry and semi-dry varieties, and some reds, although the whites are better. The grapes are grown in the volcanic soil of the La Geria region, where you can visit bodegas, and in the far north of the island, near the Mirador del Río. El Grifo is regarded as the best, but Barreto is also a reputable producer. You will find local wines in many restaurants, usually quite reasonably priced. Neighbouring Gran Canaria has some 32 wineries, and a recently introduced *denominación de origen controlada* (DOC); Monte Lentiscal, which has its own DOC, is one to look out for. Tenerife is a bigger producer, but its wines are not regularly found in restaurants.

Rum, some of which is produced at Arucas, Gran Canaria, forms the basis of Ronmiel, in which the spirit is blended with honey and lemon in a pleasant, sweet liqueur. You may also find Guindilla, a cherry liqueur from Gran Canaria, and Manzana Verde, an apple-based schnapps that is actually made in Cataluña but is widely available here.

Beer is extremely popular. You will see familiar Spanish brands such as San Miguel, and imported German and English beers, along with the Canary Islands' own Tropical and Dorada. If you want a draught beer, ask for a *caña*.

Restaurants with terraces by the sea are always popular

TO HELP YOU ORDER

Could we have a table?	**¿Nos puede dar una mesa?**
Do you have a set menu?	**¿Tiene un menú del día?**
I'd like…	**Quisiera…**

beer	**una cerveza**	milk	**leche**
bread	**pan**	mineral water	**agua mineral**
coffee	**un café**	potatoes	**patatas/**
dessert	**un postre**		**papas**
fish	**pescado**	rice	**arroz**
fruit	**fruta**	salad	**una ensalada**
glass	**un vaso**	sandwich	**un bocadillo**
ice cream	**un helado**	sugar	**azúcar**
meat	**carne**	tea	**un té**
menu	**la carta**	wine	**vino**

MENU READER

aceitunas	olives	**gambas**	prawns
albóndigas	meatballs	**langosta**	spiny lobster
almejas	baby clams	**langostino**	large prawn
anchoas	anchovies	**mariscos**	shellfish
atún	tuna	**mejillones**	mussels
bacalao	cod	**melocotón**	peach
besugo	sea bream	**navajas**	razor clams
boquerones	fresh anchovies	**ostras**	oysters
calamares	squid	**pastel**	cake
caracoles	snails	**pollo**	chicken
cerdo	pork	**pulpitos**	baby octopus
chuletas	chops	**salsa**	sauce
cocido	stew	**sepia**	cuttlefish
cordero	lamb	**ternera**	veal
entremeses	hors-d'oeuvres	**tortilla**	omelette
		trucha	trout
		uvas	grapes

PLACES TO EAT

We have used the following symbols to give an idea of the price for a three-course meal for one, including wine, cover and service:

€€€ 45 –65 euros   €€ 35–45 euros   € below 35 euros

LANZAROTE: ARRECIFE

Bodegón los Conejeros €–€€ *Avenida Rafael González Negrin 9, tel: 928 817 195*. Some great Canarian tapas are served in this wood-beamed bodega. Smoking permitted throughout. Reservations advised, especially on Friday and Saturday night.

Casa Ginory €–€€ *Calle Juan de Quesada 7, tel: 928 804 046*. In a narrow street leading from the Charco de Ginés, this small and friendly place has been here since 1965, and serves good seafood and local products such as *setas* (wild mushrooms).

Castillo de San José €€–€€€ *Puerto de Naos, tel: 928 812 321*. Excellent Canarian and international food, including imaginative puddings, in this Manrique-designed restaurant, with floor-to-ceiling windows giving views over the harbour. Smooth, efficient service – and less expensive than you might think, with a good-value tasting menu.

La Puntilla €€ *Ribera del Charco 52, tel: 928 816 042*. Over-looking the Charco, La Puntilla is an attractive place that serves excellent fish – what's on offer depends on what's been caught that day. They are also well known for their rice dishes, and there is always meat on the menu. Smoking area. Closed Sunday.

Mediterranean Altamar €€–€€€ *Arrecife Gran Hotel, Parque Islas Canarias, tel: 928 800 000*. On the 17th floor of the island's only high-rise building *(see page 29)*. The international-style food is well cooked and well presented in a somewhat formal atmosphere. The views are great.

NORTHERN LANZAROTE

ARRIETA

El Amanecer €€ *Calle La Garita 44, Playa Honda, no bookings*. A popular and highly recommended harbour-side fish restaurant, open noon–8pm. Arrive before 1pm for lunch if you want to avoid queuing for a table.

El Charcón €–€€ *Calle de Nuria s/n, tel: 928 848 110*. An attractive little place, right by the quay, with lots of outside tables. Reliably good fish dishes.

HARÍA

Dos Hermanos €€ *Plaza León y Castillo, tel: 928 835 409*. In the middle of town, this busy place serves Canarian specialities such as goat *(cabra)* and rabbit *(conejo)*, as well as seafood. Always busy at Sunday lunch time. Open 11am–8pm.

El Cortijo €€ *Calle El Palmeral 6, tel: 928 835 686*. Canarian country food, including rabbit dishes, are served in an attractive whitewashed building. Open 10am–5pm.

Restaurant Mirador del Valle €€ *Los Valles (LZ10 between Teguise and Haría), tel: 928 528 036*. Local dishes and stunning views at this *mirador* restaurant. Open 10am–5pm.

ORZOLA

Perla del Atlántico €€ *Avda Marítima 1, tel: 928 842 552*. Set on a little rocky headland, the Perla commands the bay and serves excellent fresh fish in all the usual ways – grilled *(a la plancha)* is simple and especially good. Watch the boats to Isla Graciosa come and go while you eat. Open daily 10am–6pm only.

Punta Fariones €€ *Calle de la Quemadita 10, tel: 928 842 558*. Harbour-side restaurant; fish is the speciality, but there are meat dishes as well, mostly grilled, some with *mojo* sauces.

CENTRAL LANZAROTE

COSTA TEGUISE

El Navarro €€ *Avenida del Mar 13, tel: 928 592 145*. A bit hard to find, as it's at the southwest end of the town in the Santa Rosa area, but worth it. Steaks and seafood are equally good and the puddings delight those who love puddings. Booking advisable.

El Patio €€ *Plaza del Pueblo Marinero, tel: 928 581 102*. Italian restaurant that does a good carpaccio of salmon and interesting meat dishes. Also a full range of pizzas (from a wood-fired oven) and pastas which puts it in the € bracket. There are wooden tables set out on a green terrace in the square.

La Graciosa €€€ *Hotel Gran Meliá Salinas, Avenida de las Islas Canarias, tel: 928 590 040*. If you want to dress up and really treat yourself, this is the place to come. Elegant surroundings, attentive service and excellent, international menu with wines to match. It's advisable, although not essential, to book. And don't even think about wearing shorts and a T-shirt.

Patio Canario €–€€ *Pueblo Marinero, tel: 928 346 234*. One of the few places in this resort serving genuine Canarian food. There's a wide selection, including *pimientos rellenos de bacalao* (small peppers stuffed with cod, in a creamy sauce). Has a large, wood-panelled dining room and tables outside in a quiet, shady square. Friendly, helpful staff.

MOZAGA/SAN BARTOLOMÉ

Caserio de Mozaga €€–€€€ *Mozaga, tel: 928 520 060*. The restaurant in this *casa rural* is known as one of the best places to eat on the island (no lunch on Mon or Tue). Excellent fresh ingredients and some wonderful puddings served in the attractive setting of a converted barn.

Centro de Artesanía €€ *Monumento al Campesino, San Bartolomé, tel: 928 520 136*. Authentic Canarian food: *ropa vieja* (meat, tomatoes and chickpeas), *cabra* (goat) and *conejo* (rabbit) as well as fish, in this intriguing place. You can have tapas at the bar or at outside tables, or sit in the huge, palm-decked, domed restaurant for a full meal. Lunch only. Popular with local people on Sunday, when nobody is in a hurry to leave.

PUERTO DEL CARMEN

El Sardinero € *Corner of Calle Nuestra Señora del Carmen and Avenida del Varadero, tel: 928 511 933.* This cosy little fish restaurant overlooking the harbour is highly regarded by local people and usually busy.

La Lonja de Fondeadero €€–€€€ *Plaza El Varadero s/n, tel: 928 511 377.* This is *the* place to eat fish. A large, two-storey dining room and a long wooden counter displaying tempting dishes. No outside tables, but it's right by the harbour, and they have their own excellent fish shop next door. Does a great *parillada de mariscos* (grilled mixed seafood).

La Ola €€–€€€ *Avenida de las Playas 35, tel: 928 515 081.* La Ola, part of the Lani chain that has a number of restaurants on the island, reopened in July 2011 after substantial renovation. Upstairs there are comfy white sofas and sunbeds set around a small pool by the sea; downstairs, vivid, silky cushions and low tables. Mostly Thai and Indonesian food.

Puerto Bahía €€–€€€ *Avenida del Varadero 5, tel: 928 513 793.* Another harbour-side restaurant with excellent seafood, but good grilled meats and some vegetarian dishes as well. Obliging staff and lovely views.

Puerto Viejo €€ *Avenida del Varadero s/n, tel: 928 515 265.* Excellent fish cooked by a chef known for his creativity. Also serves *Jamón Ibérico de Bellota* (the best Spanish ham, from acorn-fed Ibérico pigs). Long-standing, and frequented by local people, which is always a good sign. **El Bodegón** is a tapas bar on the premises under the same management, and on the top floor **El Asador** specialises in grilled meats.

TEGUISE

El Ryad €–€€ *Casa León, Calle León y Castillo 3, tel: 928 845 931*. Strong Middle Eastern influence, as the name suggests: kebabs, taboule, tajine chicken, etc. in an attractive old house with a patio. The adjoining café does coffee and cake as well as wine by the glass and plates of olives.

Ikarus € *Plaza 18 de Julio, tel: 928 845 332*. Cosy, red-walled rooms. Meat dishes include some excellent grilled lamb, and duck breast in a balsamic sauce. There are also lots of different varieties of pasta in this long-established venue.

La Cantina €–€€ *Calle León y Castillo 8, tel: 928 845 109*. A series of small rooms and a patio to choose from in this old Canarian house. There are various kinds of 'sharing platters' and a Thai influence – although that doesn't extend to the popular chocolate brownies. Friendly owners and pleasant atmosphere. Very busy at Sunday lunch time, when everyone's in town for the market.

Patio del Vino €€ *Palacio del Marqués, Calle Herrera y Rojas 9, tel: 928 845 773*. There's a small, elegant dining room and tables in a courtyard under trailing bougainvillea. They serve typical Canarian food and specialise in local cheese, ham and Lanzarote wines. It closes at 8pm (3pm on Sunday), so it's a lunch, tapas or early supper venue. Unusually, it is also closed on Saturday.

SOUTHERN LANZAROTE

EL GOLFO

El Golfo €–€€ *Avda del Golfo s/n, tel: 928 173 147*. Dining areas upstairs and down, inside and out. Good paella and other rice dishes, including *arroz negra* (black rice).

Mar Azul €–€€ *Avenida del Golfo 42, tel: 928 173 132*. This is a pretty blue-and-white restaurant with tables set right by the sea. It specialises, naturally, in seafood, fresh from the sea and prepared with care.

MACHER

La Cabana €€€ *LZ2 Carretera Arrecife–Uga, tel: 650 685 662*. Excellent restaurant run by an English husband and wife team. There is more meat than fish (although there's always a catch of the day); steak with black truffles and chestnut mushrooms is one of the signature dishes. Good wine list. Open Tuesday to Saturday. Reservations essential.

La Tegala €€€ *LZ2 Carretera Tías–Yaiza 60, tel: 928 524 524*. In a striking building – modern and glass-walled yet somehow atuned to the surrounding countryside – and run by the previous owner of *La Era* restaurant in Yaiza. Delicious Canarian dishes with an innovative touch. Closed Sunday.

PLAYA BLANCA

Brisa Marina €€ *Paseo Marítimo 10, tel: 928 517 006/928 517 206*. Large, green-shuttered seafront restaurant. Lots of fish, simply grilled with *mojo* sauces and a variety of rice dishes *(arroces)*. Efficient service.

El Almacén de la Sal €€ *Paseo Marítimo 12, tel: 928 517 885*. Mostly seafood but some good roast lamb, too, served in the pleasant surroundings of a converted salt warehouse by the sea.

L'Artista €€ *Calle La Tegala 18–20, tel: 928 517 578*. Just one street back from the beach, but with sea views, this attractive, green-balconied restaurant serves good Italian food, from *mare e monti* to pizzas and *tiramisú*. There's a good ambience, too.

YAIZA/TIMANFAYA

El Diablo €€ *Parque Nacional de Timanfaya, tel: 928 840 057*. Meat is barbecued over natural heat from the volcano in a large, Manrique-designed restaurant with wrap-around views.

La Casona €€€ *Calle El Rincón 11, Yaiza, tel: 928 836 262.* This attractive restaurant is set in an old winery in a *casa rural*, but is open to non-residents. It specialises in dishes made, as far as possible, from fresh local ingredients. Dinner only, except Monday when lunch is served. Closed Thursday.

La Era €€–€€€ *Trasera del Ayuntamiento, Yaiza, tel: 928 830 016.* Reopened in August 2011 under new management, so it is too early to say if this famous Manrique-designed restaurant will live up to its former reputation, but there are high hopes.

FUERTEVENTURA: PUERTO DEL ROSARIO

La Casa del Jamón €€ *La Asomada s/n, tel: 928 111 101.* On the outskirts of town, and reopened under new management in 2011, the Casa del Jamón specialises, as the name suggests, in excellent Spanish hams, but also has a varied menu and is an adherent of the 'slow food movement'.

La Marquesina Puerto €€ *Calle Pisarro 6, tel: 928 530 030.* Specialities include *pimientos rellenos* (stuffed peppers) and *sama sancochada* (sea bream in a spicy stew).

NORTHERN FUERTEVENTURA

CORRALEJO

Cofradía de Pescadores €€ *Muello Chico 5, tel: 928 867 773.* Excellent fish, as you would expect at the fishermen's co-operative. *Lubina* (bass) baked in salt may be on the menu.

El Rincón de Périco €€ *Calle General Linares 40, tel: 928 535 722.* A few metres back from the harbour, so no sea views, but the food is good. There's a *menú casero* that includes typical dishes such as *ropa vieja* and *salpicón de pescado (see page 99).*

La Marquesina €€ *Calle El Muelle, tel: 928 535 435.* By the fisherman's statue on the harbour, this friendly restaurant is always busy with customers enjoying the fresh fish.

EL COTILLO

El Roque de los Pescadores €€ *Calle de la Caleta, tel: 928 538 713*. Tables set out by the lovely harbour where you can get plates piled high with locally caught fish – even limpets, if they take your fancy.

CENTRAL FUERTEVENTURA

BETANCURIA/PÁJARA

Casa Isaítas € *Calle Guize 7, Pájara, tel: 928 161 402*. This pretty little *hostal* uses mostly local seasonal produce, which means there are lots of vegetables, hams and cheeses, but also meat and some fish dishes.

Casa Princess Arminda €–€€ *Calle Juan de Betancort 2, Betancuria, tel: 928 878 979*. This bar and restaurant opened in 2006 in a house restored by the family who have owned it for 500 years – it's said to be one of the oldest on the island. Shady bar, dining room and pretty courtyard, serving locally produced meat dishes as well as some fish and good puddings.

Casa Santa María €€ *Plaza Santa María, Betancuria, tel: 928 878 282*. In a lovingly restored 16th-century farmhouse close to the church, you can eat roast lamb *(cordero asado)*, kid *(cabrito)* and much more besides. There is also a cafeteria, serving tapas and light meals, on the other side of the road.

Don Antonio €€€ *Plaza de la Peña, La Vega del Río de las Palmas (Betancuria), tel: 928 878 757*. One of the best restaurants on the island, serving original dishes made with locally sourced ingredients in a 17th-century country-house setting. Open 10am–5pm, closed Monday.

La Fonda €€ *Calle Nuestra Señora de la Regla, Pájara, tel: 928 161 625*. Opposite the church, La Fonda serves good island food – grilled rabbit and kid *al salmorejo* (with green peppers, in a herb and garlic marinade) and other dishes with *mojo* sauces.

CALETA DE FUSTES

El Camarote €€ *Avenida El Castillo, tel: 928 859 070/928 869 073*. A pleasant place to sit and watch the world go by. The menu includes a range of local and international dishes served by helpful waiters.

La Paella €€ *Barceló Club El Castillo, Avenida El Castillo, tel: 928 163 100*. Has a terrace right on the seafront. Lots of excellent fish and, of course, paella.

O Fado €€ *Castillo Centre, tel: 928 163 369*. A Portuguese restaurant that's been here since 1996. Specialises in cod dishes, but has lots of other fish, meat and veggie options too.

SOUTHERN FUERTEVENTURA

LA PARED

Bahía La Pared €€ *Playa de La Pared, tel: 928 549 030*. Great place, right on the beach with panoramic views from the terrace. The food's good, and there's a three-course set lunch menu (**€**).

MORRO DEL JABLE/COSTA CALMA

Don Quixote €€ *Apartamentos Santa Úrsula, Costa Calma, tel: 928 875 158*. International dishes and local specialities, all well presented.

La Laja €€ *Avenida Tomás Grau (Avenida del Mar), Morro del Jable, tel: 928 542 054*. Great fish stews such as *sancocho canario*, grilled mussels with garlic, and other seafood, including some special *parrilladas* (huge plates of grilled seafood), served in a beach-side restaurant with a laid-back atmosphere.

Saavedra €€ *Avenida Tomás Grau (Avenida del Mar) Morro Jable, tel: 928 166 080/649 099 028*. This is a long established family-run place, with good fish, good atmosphere and very good prices.

A–Z TRAVEL TIPS

A Summary of Practical Information

A

ACCOMMODATION *(Alojamiento)*

Most accommodation on Lanzarote is in the three major resorts: Puerto del Carmen, Costa Teguise and Playa Blanca. Self-catering apartments are more common than hotel rooms, and are good value. Elsewhere, there is not a great deal of choice, although there are several acceptable hotels in Arrecife, and in the interior of both islands there is a growing number of *casas rurales* – rural properties that have been converted into small hotels or renovated and rented as self-catering accommodation. For information, contact ww.ruralvillas.com. You will not find budget accommodation in the resorts. Similarly in Fuerteventura, nearly all accommodation is in the main resorts *(see Recommended Hotels, pages 135–42)*.

Hotels are rated from one-star to five-star Gran Lujo (GL). Prices within the categories may vary considerably. Breakfast is usually included in the rate. Package holidays are the most economical, offering accommodation in large, comfortable hotels and self-catering apartments, some known as aparthotels. It is wise to book in advance, especially around Christmas, Easter and July to August.

I would like a single/ double room with/without bathroom and toilet/shower	**Quisiera una habitación sencilla/doble con/sin baño/ducha**
What's the rate per night?	**¿Cuál es el precio por noche?**
Is breakfast included?	**¿Está incluido el desayuno?**

AIRPORTS *(Aeropuertos)*

Lanzarote's Arrecife's **Guacimeta** airport (ACE) has two terminals. Terminal 1 services international flights. Thursday is 'change over' day in the resorts, which means the departures section can be very busy and best avoided if possible. The airport is about 6km (4 miles) west of Arrecife. There is a bus service to Arrecife about every half-hour (No. 22 or 23 at weekends; €1.20; tel: 928 811 522).

A taxi from the airport to Arrecife costs about €12, to Puerto del Carmen around €15, to Costa Teguise €20 and to Playa Blanca €40, although may be more expensive if reserved in advance.
Arrecife airport information, tel: 928 846 000.
Taxi reservations, tel: 630 207 305, www.lanzarotetaxi.com.

Fuerteventura's modern and efficient airport **El Matorral** (FUE) is about 7km (4 miles) south of Puerto del Rosario, about 9 km (6 miles) north of Caleta de Fustes. Bus No. 3 runs via Puerto del Rosario to Caleta de Fustes every half-hour (€1.80; tel: 928 852 166). A taxi from the airport to the capital costs about €12, to Caleta de Fustes about €15.
Fuerteventura airport information, tel: 928 860 600.
Taxi service, tel: 928 855 432/619 845 414.

B

BICYCLE HIRE (Bicicletas de alquiler)

Road bikes, mountain bikes and scooters can be hired in most of the resorts (see What to Do, page 87).

BUDGETING FOR YOUR TRIP

Accommodation: Rates for two sharing a double room in high season (July–August) can range from as low as €60 in a basic apartment or at a *pensión* or hostel (although there aren't many of these) to as much as €400 at a top-of-the-range five-star hotel. A pleasant three-star hotel will cost in the range of €100–€150. Rates drop considerably out of season, except at Christmas and Easter.

Attractions: The major attractions such as the Manrique sites and Cueva de los Verdes charge around €8; smaller museums around €5. More expensive are the family attractions such as the Jardín

Tropical and the Aquapark (around €4, reductions for children).
Bike hire: between €10 and €12 a day, depending on the bike and the number of days for which it is hired.
Buses: eg. Arrecife to Puerto del Carmen or Costa Teguise €1.20.
Car hire: Including comprehensive insurance and tax, rates are around €30–40 a day from the big international companies; you get a better deal if you book for a week *(see page 119)*.
Getting there: Air fares vary enormously, with those from the UK to Lanzarote ranging between £100 in November to £400 in August (€115–€460), with spring and early-summer flights somewhere in between. From the US, flights cost around $1,000. To Fuerteventura they range between £100 in November to around £280 (€115–320) in August – the lower summer price compared to Lanzarote due to the fact that there are *only* budget flights to Fuerteventura. Cheapest flights are available via the internet, and booked well in advance, or by taking a chance on a last-minute offer.
Meals and drinks: The cheap, three-course set meal called the *menú del día* is found less on these two islands than it is in most other parts of Spain. The average price of a three-course à la carte meal, including house wine, will be about €35 per person, but you can pay a lot less. At top restaurants you may pay nearly twice that.
Petrol: still cheap by UK standards – around €0.94–€1 a litre.
Taxis: Prices are controlled, and reasonable. From Lanzarote airport to Puerto del Carmen the fare is around €15, as is the fare from Fuerteventura airport to Caleta de Fustes.

C

CAMPING

There are two official campsites on Lanzarote (June–Sept only), but they do not offer much in the way of space or facilities:
• Camping El Salao, Isla Graciosa, tel: 928 845 985/842 000. Basic facilities (toilets/showers); tents only; no fires or barbecues; free.

• Camping de Papagayo, Playa Blanca, tel: 928 173 724; €4 for a small tent pitch, €7 for larger pitches.

On Fuerteventura there are no official campsites, but rough camping is tolerated in some places; check with the local tourist office.

CAR HIRE *(Coches de alquiler;* see also DRIVING)

You must be over 21, sometimes 24, to hire a car, and have held a icence for at least 12 months. You need your passport and a credit card. It is not easy to find a vehicle with automatic transmission. There are dozens of local companies in the resorts, and these tend to be cheaper, but check that cars are reliable and make sure you know what insurance you're getting: comprehensive with full damage waiver *(todo riesgo)* is more expensive but worthwhile. It may be cheaper to hire a car via the internet before you leave home. Cabrera Medina (Lanzarote airport tel: 928 846 276, www.cabrera medina.com) is the biggest and most respected of the local companies, with numerous outlets in the resorts, in Arrecife and at the airport. The big international companies all have offices at both islands' airports and in the resorts.

• Avis: Lanzarote airport tel: 928 846 245, www.avis.com.
• Europcar: Lanzarote airport tel: 928 84260, www.europcar.com.
• Hertz: Lanzarote airport tel: 928 846190, www.hertz.com.

I'd like to rent a car for one day/week	**Quisiera alquilar un coche por un día/una semana**
Please include full insurance.	**Haga el favor de incluir el seguro a todo riesgo.**

CLIMATE

The islands have an average annual temperature of 20°C (68°F), with mid-summer temperatures soaring to 30°C (86°F). There is very little rain – what there is mostly falls October–January.

CLOTHING

Light summer clothes, sandals and a swimsuit are all you need much of the time, but bring a sweater or jacket for cooler evenings and windy boat rides, and strong shoes if you want to do any walking. A jacket for men and a smart dress for women is appreciated, but not obligatory, in more expensive restaurants. Don't offend local sensibilities by wearing swimwear or skimpy clothing in city streets, museums or churches, although you can get away with almost anything in resorts.

CRIME AND SAFETY

Crime rates are not high, but there is some opportunistic bag-snatching and pickpocketing in busy tourist areas. Robberies from cars are the most prevalent, so never leave anything of value in your vehicle. Use the safe deposit box in your room for valuables, including your passport (carrying a photocopy is a good idea). Burglaries of holiday apartments do occur, too, so keep doors and windows locked when you are out. You must report all thefts to the local police within 24 hours for your own insurance purposes.

| I want to report a theft. | **Quiero denunciar un robo.** |

D

DISABLED TRAVELLERS

Arrecife and Fuerteventura airports and most modern hotels have wheelchair access and facilities for travellers with disabilities, but, generally speaking, facilities elsewhere are not good. For general information, consult the online *Able Magazine*, tel: 0141 419 0044, www.ablemagazine.co.uk. Tourism for All, tel: 0845 124 9971, www.tourismforall.org.uk also provides information.

DRIVING

Driving conditions: Main roads are generally well surfaced and signposted – although signage in the north of Lanzarote is a bit arbitrary. There are lots of roundabouts, but no traffic lights outside Arrecife. Drive on the right, pass on the left, yield right of way to vehicles coming from your left on roundabouts, but give way to vehicles coming from the right at junctions. Use your horn when approaching sharp bends. In rural areas you may come across a very slow tractor or a large pothole – even goats, in Fuerteventura.

Speed limits: 110km/h (74mph) on motorways, 100km/h (62mph) on dual carriageways, 90km/h (52mph) on primary roads, 50km/h (30mph) in built-up areas; 40km/h (25mph) in residential areas.

There are only a couple of stretches of motorway, around each of the capital cities and their airports, and they are toll-free.

Traffic and parking: In Arrecife traffic can be heavy, parking difficult and the one-way system confusing. Early afternoon is a good time to get in and out of town, and you are more likely to find a parking space. In Puerto del Rosario parking is rarely a problem. Elsewhere there are few traffic jams or parking problems.

It is an offence to park facing the traffic. Don't park on white or yellow lines. Blue lines indicate pay-and-display parking areas.

Petrol: Petrol is cheaper than in the UK and the rest of Europe. Unleaded is *sin plomo*. A few of the larger petrol stations *(gasolineras)* are open 24 hours; most accept credit cards. In the interior of both islands there are fewer petrol stations , so don't run too low on fuel.

Regulations: Always carry your driving licence with you. Seat belts are compulsory. Children under 10 must travel in the rear. Don't use a mobile phone. Obviously, you should never drink and drive.

Traffic police: Armed Civil Guards (Guardia Civil) patrol the roads on motorcycles. In towns the municipal police handle traffic control. If you are fined for a traffic offence, you may have to pay on the spot or take your fine to the local town hall.

aparcamiento	parking
desviación	detour
obras	roadworks
peatones	pedestrians
peligro	danger
salida de camiones	truck exit
senso único	one way

Useful expressions:

¿Se puede aparcar aquí?	Can I park here?
Llénelo, por favor.	Fill the tank please.
Ha habido un accidente.	There has been an accident.

E

ELECTRICITY *(Corriente eléctrica)*

220 volts is standard, with continental-style, two-pin sockets. Adaptors are available in UK shops and at airports. North American 110V appliances need a transformer.

EMBASSIES AND CONSULATES *(Embajadas y consulados)*

Australia: (in Madrid), tel: 913 536 600.
Ireland: Calle León y Castillo 195, Las Palmas, tel: 928 297 728.
South Africa: Honorary Consulate, c/o Calle Albareda 54, Las Palmas, tel: 928 265 452.
UK: Calle Luis Morote 6, Las Palmas, tel: 092 109 356, .
US: Calle Martínez Escobar 3, Las Palmas, tel: 928 271 259.

EMERGENCIES *(Urgencias;* see also EMBASSIES, HEALTH, POLICE)

General emergencies:	112
National police:	091
Local police:	092

Guardia Civil:	062
Traffic police:	928 315 575
Ambulance:	061
Fire brigade:	080

Police!	¡Policía!
Help!	¡Socorro!
Fire!	¡Fuego!
Stop!	¡Deténgase!

G

GAY AND LESBIAN TRAVELLERS

The people of the Canary Islands generally have a tolerant attitude and there a number of gay bars in the resorts. For information, visit www.gayinspain.com/canarias or http://lanzarotegayguide.com.

GETTING THERE

By air: There are numerous budget airline flights direct from most UK airports to **Lanzarote** (easyJet, Ryanair, etc.). The flight time is about four hours. There are scheduled flights from London Heathrow (eg Iberia, www.iberia.com) that go via Madrid and/or Gran Canaria, which makes it a long journey.

There are not so many direct flight options to **Fuerteventura**, but Thomas Cook (www.flythomascook.com) has a number of direct flights; flights operated by a number of other airlines can be found through www.flydeals.co.uk.

At present there are no direct flights from the US, but several transatlantic carriers (American Airlines, Iberia, Air Europa), have flights via Madrid; the overall flight time is about 12 hours. Connections can also be made via London airports; check with a travel agency, or visit www.opodo.com.

Inter-island flights are operated by Binter Airlines (tel: 902 391 392, www.bintercanarias.es), for information.The flight from Las Palmas de Gran Canaria to Arrecife takes about 45 minutes.

By ship: The Trasmediterránea ferry company runs a weekly service from Cádiz to Las Palmas de Gran Canaria and from there there are regular services to Puerto del Rosario and Arrecife (tel: 902 454 645 or check www.trasmediterranea.es). Naviera Armas (tel: 902 456 500 or 928 517 912 in Playa Blanca, www.naviera-armas.com) has services three times a week from Gran Canaria to Fuerteventura and to Lanzarote. Naviera Armas runs frequent ferries from Playa Blanca, Lanzarote, to Corralejo, Fuerteventura; crossings take about 35 minutes. The Fred Olsen Shipping Line, tel: 902 100 107 or 928 495 040, www.fredolsen.es, runs the *Bocayna Express* catamaran from Playa Blanca, Lanzarote, to Corralejo, Fuerteventura; journey time about 20 minutes. Fred Olsen sailings are more expensive, but the advantage for visitors not based in the south of the island is that there is a free bus service from Arrecife and Puerto del Carmen, which also calls at the airport.

H

HEALTH AND MEDICAL CARE

Non-EU visitors should always have private medical insurance, and athough there are reciprocal arrangements between EU countries, it is advisable for UK citizens and other member nations to do the same, because the arrangements do not cover all eventualities. The European Health Insurance Card (EHIC) entitles UK citizens to reciprocal medical care. You can apply for one online (www.ehic.org.uk), by phone (tel: 0845 606 2030) or by picking up a form at a main post office. Only treatment provided under a state scheme is covered, so make sure the practitioner is working within the Spanish Health Service. Leave a photocopy of the card with the hospital or doctor. Dental treatment is not available under this system. Hotel receptionists or private clinics will be able to recommend dentists.

Hospitals: The main hospital in Arrecife is Hospital Insular, Juan de Quesada s/n (Puerto de Naos), tel: 928 810 500.

In Puerto del Rosario: Hospital General, Carretera General del Aeropuerto Km 1, tel: 928 862 000 or 920 531 799.

Red Cross (Cruz Roja): Lanzarote: tel: 928 812 222; Fuerteventura tel: 928 852 222.

Private clinics: In the resorts on both islands there are private clinics where you will have to pay for treatment on the spot and reclaim it on your medical insurance. Most have English-speaking staff.

Lanzarote:

Branches of Clínica Lanzarote offer 24-hour service. The 24-hour emergency number is tel: 900 100 450. Clinics are located at:

- Costa Teguise: Avda Islas Canarias, tel: 928 591 014.
- Puerto del Carmen: Avda de las Playas 5, tel: 928 513 171.
- Playa Blanca: Hotel Lanzarote Park, Limones, tel: 928 519 039.

Fuerteventura:

- Caleta de Fustes: Salus, Centro Comercial el Castillo, Local 15, tel: 928 163 445.
- Corralejo: Centro Médico Brisamar, Calle Nuestra Señora del Carmen, tel: 928 536 402.
- Costa Calma: Costa Calma Medical Centre, tel: 928 875 300.
- Morro Jable: Centro Médico Morro Jable, Edificio Don Carlos, Local A, Playa Matorral, tel: 928 545 070/928 541 543.

Farmacias: Most problems visitors experience are due to too much sun, too much alcohol, or food they are unused to. These problems can often be dealt with by *farmacias* (chemists), identified by a green cross. Spanish pharmacists are highly trained and can often dispense medicines over the counter that would need a prescription in the UK. They are open during normal shopping hours, and one in each town, the *farmacia de guardia,* remains open all night. Its location is posted in the window of other *farmacias* and in local papers.

Where's the nearest (all-night) chemist?	¿Dónde está la farmacia (de guardia) más cercana?
I need a doctor/dentist	Necesito un médico/dentista
sunburn	quemadura del sol
sunstroke	una insolación
a fever	fiebre
an upset stomach	molestias de estómago

L

LANGUAGE (Idioma, lenguaje)

The Spanish spoken in the Canary Islands is slightly different from that of the mainland. A number of Latin American words and expressions are used. The most common are *guagua* (pronounced *wah-wah*), meaning bus, and *papa* (potato). In tourist areas basic English, German and some French is spoken, or at least understood. The *Berlitz Spanish Phrasebook & Dictionary* covers most of the situations you may encounter.

M

MAPS (Planos)

Most tourist offices, and some of the larger hotels, will give you free maps, which should be sufficient, and hire car agencies usually provide a basic road map. If you want something more detailed, you can find road maps in most gift/souvenir shops and supermarkets for around €3–4.

Do you have a map of the city/island?	¿Tiene un plano de la ciudad/isla?

MEDIA

Radio and television *(radio; televisión)*: Many hotels have satellite TV with several stations in various languages, including CNN. TV Canarias is a local station which includes some English-language news and tourist information in its programming. English-language radio stations include Radio FM 95.3 Mhz, Power FM 91.2 Mhz and Waves FM 96.8 Mhz.

Newspapers and magazines *(periódicos; revistas)*: Major British and German tabloids are on sale in the resorts on the day of publication, but English broadsheet newspapers are a bit more scarce. British and German magazines are widely available.

The online English-language Island Connections (www.island-connections.eu) has island news and tourist information but concentrates mainly on Gran Canaria and Tenerife.

For anyone who speaks Spanish, the island newspapers are *Canarias7* and *La Provincia*. Both of these contain listings of events so they can be useful, even if your Spanish is very sketchy, but, again, they do concentrate more on Gran Canaria and Tenerife.

MONEY *(Dinero)*

Currency: The monetary unit in the Canary Islands, as throughout Spain, is the euro, abbreviated €. Banknotes are available in denominations of €500, 200, 100, 50, 20, 10 and 5. The euro is subdivided into 100 cents, and there are coins available for €1 and €2 and for 50, 20, 10, 5, 2 and 1 cent.

Currency exchange: Banks are the preferred place to exchange currency, but *casas de cambio* also change money, as do some travel agencies, and these stay open outside banking hours. Larger hotels may change guests' money, but the rate is less advantageous. Banks and exchange offices pay less for cash than for traveller's cheques. Always take your passport when changing money.

Credit cards: Major international cards are widely recognised, although smaller businesses tend to prefer cash. Visa/Eurocard/

MasterCard are most generally accepted. Credit and debit cards, with a PIN number, are also useful for obtaining euros from ATMs, which are to be found in all towns and resorts. They offer the most convenient way of obtaining cash, and will usually give you the best exchange rate, sometimes indicating the current rate on the screen.

Traveller's cheques: Hotels, shops, restaurants and travel agencies all cash traveller's cheques, and so do banks, where you will probably get a better rate (you will need your passport). It is advisable to cash small amounts at a time, keeping some of your funds in cheques in the hotel safe.

Where's the nearest bank/ currency exchange office?	**¿Dónde está el banco más cercano/la casa de cambio más cercana?**
I want to change some dollars/pounds	**Quiero cambiar dólares/ libres esterlina**
Do you accept traveller's cheques?	**¿Acepta usted cheques de viajero?**
Can I pay with this credit card?	**¿Puedo pagar con esta tarjeta de crédito?**

O

OPENING TIMES *(Horario comercial)*

Banks usually open Monday to Friday 9am–2pm; large ones may also open on Saturday. Shops and offices are usually open Monday to Saturday, 9am–1 or 1.30pm, 4–8pm (although some close on Saturday afternoon). Large supermarkets may stay open all day and until 10pm, as do many shops in the tourist resorts, and some also open on Sunday. Post offices open Monday to Saturday 9am–2pm.

P

POLICE *(Policías;* see also EMERGENCIES)

There are three police forces in Gran Canaria, as in the rest of Spain. The green-uniformed Guardia Civil (Civil Guard) is the main force. Each town also has its own Policía Municipal (municipal police), whose uniform can vary but is mostly blue and grey. The third force, the Cuerpo Nacional de Policía, is a national anti-crime unit that sports a light brown uniform. All police officers are armed. Spanish police are strict but courteous to foreign visitors.

National police:	091 or 928 812 350/902 102 112
Guardia Civil:	062

Where's the nearest police station?	¿Dónde está la comisaría más cercana?

POST OFFICES *(Correos)*

Post offices usually open Monday to Saturday 8.30am–2pm; some open in the afternoon from 4–7pm, but it is better not to count on it. They are for mail, not telephone calls. The main post office in Arrecife is at Avenida de la Marina 8. In Costa Teguise, it's in the Centro Comercial Maretas on Avenida Islas Canarias, almost opposite the police station. In Puerto del Carmen, it's on Avenida Juan Carlos I s/n; in Playa Blanco, Avenida El Correlillo s/n. On Fuerteventura, Puerto del Rosario's post office is at Avenida Primero de Mayo 58; in Morro Jable, the post office can be found on Calle Buenavista s/n.

Stamps *(sellos)* are also sold at any tobacconist *(estanco)* and by most shops selling postcards, including supermarkets in the resorts. Mailboxes are painted yellow. If one of the slots is marked *extranjero,* it is for letters abroad.

| Where is the (nearest) post office? | ¿Dónde está la oficina de correos (más cercana)? |
| A stamp for this letter/ postcard, please | Por favor, un sello para esta carta/tarjeta |

PUBLIC HOLIDAYS *(Días festivos)*

1 January	*Año Nuevo*	New Year's Day
6 January	*Día de los Reyes*	Epiphany
1 May	*Día del Trabajo*	Labour Day
30 May	*Día de las Islas Canarias*	Canary Islands' Day
16 July	*Nuestra Señora del Carmen*	Our Lady of Carmen
25 July	*Santiago Apóstol*	St James' Day
15 August	*Asunción*	Assumption Day
12 October	*Día de la Hispanidad*	National Day
1 November	*Todos los Santos*	All Saints' Day
6 December	*Día de la Constitución*	Constitution Day
8 December	*Inmaculada Concepción*	Immaculate Conception
25 December	*Navidad*	Christmas Day

Movable dates:

Carnaval Officially pre-Lent but different towns celebrate at different times so dates do not clash.

Jueves Santo Maundy Thursday.

Viernes Santo Good Friday.

Corpus Christi Corpus Christi (mid-June).

T

TAXES *(Impuestos)*

A sales tax, the Impuesto Generalisado Indirecto Canario (IGIC) is levied on all bills at a rate of 5 percent. The tax may be included in the price you are quoted for hotel rooms, but usually it is not.

TELEPHONES *(Teléfono)*

Phone booths *(kioskos)* accept coins and cards *(tarjetas telefónicas)*, available from tobacconists, hotels and machines that you will see in all the shopping centres – they come in denominations of €5 and €10. Instructions in English and area/country codes are displayed clearly in phone booths. International calls are expensive, so have a plentiful supply of coins or use a card. *Cabinas* or *locutorios* – cabins where you make a call and then pay at a desk afterwards – are a more convenient way of making long-distance calls. Calling from your hotel room is expensive, as it is anywhere in the world.

Making and receiving mobile phone calls is expensive but it is probably not worth getting a Spanish SIM card unless you are staying a long time or are going to be making a large number of calls.

For international calls, wait for the dial tone, then dial 00, wait for a second tone and dial the country code, area code (minus any initial zero) and the number. **International Operator**: 025.

Country codes: Australia 61, Ireland 353, New Zealand 64, UK 44, US and Canada 1.

Telephone codes for the Canary Islands (which must always be dialled, even for local calls): Gran Canaria, Lanzarote and Fuerteventura 928; Tenerife, El Hierro, La Gomera and La Palma 922.

TIME ZONES

The time in the Canaries is the same as in the UK, Greenwich Mean Time, but one hour behind the rest of Europe, including Spain, and five hours ahead of New York. Like the rest of Europe, the islands adopt summer time (putting the clocks forward by an hour) from the end of March through to the end of September.

TIPPING *(Propinas)*

A service charge is sometimes included in restaurant bills (look for the words *servicio incluído*). If it is not included, then add around

10 percent, which is also the usual tip for taxi drivers and hairdressers. In bars, customers usually leave a few coins, rounding up the bill. A hotel porter will appreciate €1 for carrying heavy bags to your room; tip hotel maids acording to your length of stay.

TOILETS *(Servicios, baños)*

Public conveniences are rare. The proprietors of some bars and restaurants do not mind if you drop in to use their facilities, but it is polite to buy something, even if it is only a bottle of water. Others keep the key behind the bar to make sure their toilets are not used by the general public or, if they are, that users pay a small sum.

Where are the lavatories?   **¿Dónde están los servicios?**

TOURIST INFORMATION OFFICES
(Oficinas de información turística)

Tourist offices abroad:
• **Australia:** dealt with by the National Tourist Office of Spain, 541 Orchard Road, 09–04 Liat Towers, Singapore 238881, tel: 65-737 3008, email: singapore@tourspain.es.
• **Canada:** 2 Bloor Street West, Suite 3402, Toronto, Ontario M4W 3E2, tel: 1416-961 3131, www.tourspaintoronto.on.ca.
• **Ireland:** 1–3 Westmoreland Street, Dublin 2, tel: 01-6350 200.
• **UK:** Spanish National Tourist Office, 79 New Cavendish Street, London W1W 6SB (appointments only), tel: 020 7486 8077, information line tel: 0870-850 6599, www.spain.info.
• **US:** 666 Fifth Avenue, New York, NY 10103, tel: 212 265 8822, www.okspain.org.
Tourist offices on the islands: (open approx. 9.30am–1.30pm)
Lanzarote:
• Airport: tel: 928 820 704.

- Arrecife: Parque José Ramírez Cerdá, tel: 928 811 762/813 174.
- Costa Teguise: Avenida de las Islas Canarias, tel: 928 592 542.
- Playa Blanca: El Varadero s/n, tel: 928 519 018/928 518 150.
- Puerto del Carmen: Avenida de las Playas s/n (next to the Fundación Manrique shop), tel: 928 15 337/928 513 351.

Fuerteventura:
- Airport: tel: 928 860 604 and 928 866 235.
- Caleta de Fustes: Avenida Juan Ramón Soto Morales 10, Centro Comercial Castillo, tel: 928 163 286.
- Corralejo: Plaza Grande, tel: 928 866 235/928 537 183.
- Morro Jable: Centro Comercial Cosmo, Avenida El Saladar, Local 88, tel: 928 540 776.
- Puerto del Rosario: Calle Almirante Lallermand 1, tel: 928 530 844.

TRANSPORT *(Transporte)*

There is no train service on either island. The **bus services** are cheap and reliable but really only useful for getting from the two islands' capital cities to the main resorts. Buses between towns are infrequent, although there are some useful services in the south of Fuerteventura.

Lanzarote: tel: 928 811 522; www.arrecifebus.com.

Fuerteventura: tel: 928 850 951; www.maxoratabus.com.

(For inter-island ferries and flights, *see page 124*.)

Taxis: The letters SP *(servicio público)* on the front and rear bumpers of a car indicate that it is a taxi. It may also have a green light in the front windscreen or a green sign indicating '*libre*' when it is free. There is no shortage of taxis in urban areas and resorts. Fares are metered, but for longer, out-of-town journeys you may feel happier if you agree an approximate fare in advance. Taxis are good value: the fare from the airport to Puerto del Carmen is €15, to Costa Teguise €20, and to Playa Blanca €40. On Fuerteventura, the fare from the airport to Caleta de Fustes is

around €15, and around €40 to Corralejo.
Lanzarote: Lanzarote Taxi, tel: 928 800 806,
Fuerteventura: PlusCar, tel: 928 827 055.

V

VISAS AND ENTRY REQUIREMENTS *(Aduana)*

Citizens of EU countries, the US, Canada, Ireland, Australia and
New Zealand need only a valid passport. No inoculations are re-
quired. The islands are part of the EU but there is a restriction on
duty-free goods that can be brought back to the UK. The allowance
is 200 cigarettes or 50 cigars or 250g tobacco; 1 litre spirits over 22
percent or 2 litres under 22 percent, and 2 litres of wine.

W

WATER *(Agua)*

The islands suffer from water shortage, so try not to waste it. Don't
drink tap water. Inexpensive bottled water is available everywhere.
Con gas is sparkling, *sin gas* is still. If you are self-catering you cn
buy 5-litre bottles very cheaply in suspermarkets.

WEBSITES AND INTERNET ACCESS

www.ecoturismocanarias.com natural parks and rural tourism.
www.rural-villas.com for attractive rural villas and apartments.
www.fuerteventura.com helpful site for general information.
www.lanzaroteguidebook.com lots of general information.
www.turismolanzarote.com official Lanzarote tourism site.

Internet: There are internet cafés in all the resorts, usually in the
big commercial centres, although they tend to come and go. Most
hotels now have internet access in their public areas and some now
offer free Wi-fi as well.

Recommended Hotels

Most accommodation on both islands is concentrated in the resorts. Elsewhere, there is not a great deal of choice, although there are some delightful *casas rurales* (rural hotels) in the island interiors (check www.rural-villas.com), and several very acceptable ones in Arrecife. You will find very little budget accommodation in the resorts. Self-catering apartments are ubiquitous and good value. Most are in holiday complexes, some called aparthotels, and usually offer hotel facilities such as a pool, restaurant, etc. You can also rent an apartment on a bed-and-breakfast or half-board basis.

Prices are for two sharing a double room, or a one-bedroomed apartment, in high season (July–August and Christmas/New Year; some rural *casas* charge high-season rates in autumn). Breakfast is usually included in the rates. Tax (IGIC) is extra if you book independently, but included if you book a package. Prices are approximate only, and if you take a package deal you will usually pay considerably less.

€€€€	over €200
€€€	€120–200
€€	€70–120
€	below €70

LANZAROTE: ARRECIFE

Arrecife Gran Hotel €€–€€€ *Parque Islas Canarias, tel: 928 800 000, www.arrecifehoteles.com.* This 17-storey hotel, completely renovated, is smart and glossy, with a conference room, shops, a hairdressing salon, swimming pool, sauna and gym, underground parking and stunning views from the restaurant/bar on the top floor and from many of the well-furnished rooms and suites.

Lancelot €–€€ *Calle Mancomunidad 9, tel: 928 805 099, www.hotellancelot.com.* A pleasant modern hotel right by the Reducto beach, with babysitting services, a pool and a restaurant with sea views. A convenient base for a short stay. Has some good half-board offers.

HARÍA

Casa Villa Lola y Juan €€ *Calle Fajardo 16, Haría, tel: 928 835 256, www.villalolayjuan.com.* In the greenest part of Lanzarote, this agreeable little hotel is surrounded by fruit trees and vines. One villa and two apartments, each with terrace. There's a pool and a solarium.

Finca La Corona €€–€€€ *Calle La Rosita, Yé (Haría), tel: 902 363 318.* Set beween Monte la Corona and the Mirador del Río, with fantastic views. There are six apartments in the main house and a converted stable block, all comfortably furnished in rustic style, with white walls and tiled floors. There's a heated pool, a children's pool, a sauna and jacuzzi. Can be rented as a whole house.

La Ermita €€ *Máguez (Haría), tel: 928 842 535, mobile: 659 021 447, www.casalaermita.com.* Four simply furnished apartments, a communal patio and saltwater pool, conveniently situated for visiting the Manrique attractions in the north of the island, and about 10 minutes' drive from Playa la Garrita and Arrieta. Bikes for hire.

ISLA GRACIOSA

Apartamentos El Sombrerito € *Calle Sirena 71, Caleta del Sebo, mobile: 696 942 874, www.elsombrerito.com.* Seven simple apartments a stone's throw from the harbour. Perfect peace.

Pensión Girasol € *Calle García Escámez 1, Caleta del Sebo, tel: 928 842 118.* Right by the harbour, there are eight double rooms to rent in this family-run *pension* and restaurant.

COSTA TEGUISE

Apartamentos Celeste € *Avda de las Islas Canarias 21–25, tel: 928 591 720, www.apartmentsceleste.com.* Simple, pleasant apartments in an attractive building that is part of the pretty Pueblo Marinero, the nicest area in the resort. Very close to the beach.

Barceló La Galea €€€ *Paseo Marítimo s/n, tel: 928 590 551, www.barcelolagalea.com*. Comfortable, well-equipped studios and apartments arranged around a pool in an attractive low-rise complex, built in traditional, Manrique-approved style by the beach at the west end of Playa de las Cucharas. All-inclusive packages available.

Gran Meliá Salinas €€€€ *Avenida de las Islas Canarias s/n, tel: 902 144 440, from the UK: 0808 234 1953, www.gran-melia-salinas. com*. Right on the beach, this hotel has luxurious rooms, faultless service, and a wonderful lobby and atrium created by Manrique, with pools, tropical foliage and statuary. Hibiscus flowers are scattered everywhere, even in the marble-walled toilets. Such pleasures do not come cheap.

Lanzarote Gardens €€–€€€ *Avda de las Islas Canarias 13, tel: 928 590 100, www.hotelh10lanzarotegardens.com*. One- and two-bedroomed fully serviced apartments in attractive gardens grouped around two pools, just back from Playa de las Cucharas. All rooms have balconies. Restaurant, poolside bar. Children's entertainment every evening, and a small playground and children's pool area. Efficient, multilingual staff. Also offers full-board packages.

MOZAGA/SAN BARTOLOMÉ

Caserio de Mozaga €€ *Mozaga, tel: 928 520 060, www. caseriodemozaga.com*. An 18th-century farmhouse with a flowerfilled courtyard and eight double rooms with tiled floors, woodbeamed ceilings and traditional furniture. Tradition is complemented with modernity: air-conditioning and internet access in the rooms. Great breakfasts and an excellent restaurant, open to the public *(see page 108)*.

Finca de la Florida €€ *El Islote 90, San Bartolomé, tel: 928 521 124, www.hotelfincadelaflorida.com*. In the wine-producing area of La Geria, about 2km (1 mile) from the Monumento del Campesino, this attractive blue-and-white hotel offers 15 comfortably furnished double rooms and one suite. Gym, sauna, pool, jacuzzi, and tennis and mountain bikes are available.

PUERTO DEL CARMEN

Balcón del Mar € *Calle Reina Sofía 23, tel: 928 513 725/928 510 726, www.balcondelmar.com.* These pleasant apartments and bungalows are located up a hill from the beach and harbour. It's a bit of a hike, but it is right by a bus stop and set among gardens, with two pools, splendid views and easy parking.

La Geria €€–€€€ *Calle Jupiter 5, Playa de los Pocillos, tel: 928 510 441, www.hipotels.com.* Pleasant four-storey hotel at the quieter end of the resort. Rooms have sea views to the side, or garden/pool views. There is a landscaped pool area.

Los Cocoteros €€ *Avda de las Playas 17, tel: 928 510 361, www.loscocoteroslanzarote.com.* Pleasant white block with Gaudíesque chimneys. Well-equipped serviced apartments with patios. Most have sea views.

Los Fariones €€€€ *Calle Roque del Este 1, tel: 928 510 175, www.farioneshotels.com.* This huge, comfortable 1960s hotel is right beside the beach at the harbour end of the resort, set in lush gardens. Pool and tennis court. Opposite is the even smarter Fariones Suites Hotel.

Los Jameos Playa €€€–€€€€ *Playa de los Pocillos s/n, tel: 928 511 717, www.los-jameos-playa.es.* A large, light hotel with Canarian-style balconies in the spacious reception area. Rooms built around a series of airy white-painted courtyards.

Vik Hotel San Antonio €€–€€€ *Avenida de las Playas 84, tel: 928 514 200, www.vikhotels.com.* Located at the point between Playa Grande and Playa de los Pocillos, where the road becomes quieter and more residential. It looks rather clinical from outside, but it is extremely comfortable and well run. Most of the rooms have sea views, but check when you book.

PLAYA BLANCA

Casa del Embajador €€€ *Calle La Tegala 30, tel: 928 519 191, www.hotelcasadelembajador.com*. Unusual in Playa Blanca, this is a family-run hotel in an old house that once belonged to a diplomat (hence the name). Right by the beach, it has just 12 rooms and one suite, all well furnished and decorated. There's lots of atmosphere and wonderful views across to Fuerteventura.

Hotel Volcán Lanzarote €€€–€€€€ *Urbanización Castillo de Águila s/n, tel: 928 519 185, www.hotelvolcanlanzarote.com*. Spacious and luxurious, this new hotel, which overlooks the Marina Rubicón yacht harbour, has 255 rooms, all with terrraces or balconies, located in 20 separate buildings. There are three conference rooms, five restaurants, several bars, four pools, a gym and spa. Caters to business people and holiday-makers.

Lanzarote Princess €€€ *Calle Maciot s/n, tel: 928 517 108, www.hotelh10lanzaroteprincess.com*. Part of the reliable H10 chain, this hotel is set back a couple of hundred metres from Playa Dorada beach. The air-conditioned rooms all have terraces or balconies. There are three restaurants, two pools, tennis court, volleyball, children's facilities and entertainment.

Princess Yaiza €€€€ *Avenida Papagayo s/n, tel: 928 519 222, www.princesayaiza.com*. Right on the beach, this smart hotel has a strong Hispano-Arabic theme to the architecture. Five restaurants offer Japanese, Italian and Mexican food, among other styles. There's a spa, gym, pools, squash, tennis, and Kikoland, a children's playground. Minimum four nights' stay.

Timanfaya Palace €€–€€€ *Urbanización Montaña Roja s/n, tel: 928 517 676, www.hotelh10timanfayapalace.com*. This hotel on

Playa Flamingo has Arabic-style architecture, comfortable rooms, billiards/snooker, gym and all-weather tennis court, plus babysitting services, children's play area; free Wi-fi in public areas.

UGA/YAIZA

Casa El Morro €€–€€€ *Uga, tel: 928 830 392, www.casaelmorro lanzarote.com.* Perched on a hillside, this attractive complex offers modern comfort in a traditional 18th-century building. There are six individually decorated *casitas* surounded by palms and bougainvillea, ranged round a courtyard; small pool, views over volcanic hills and lots of peace and tranquillity.

Casona de Yaiza €€€ *Calle El Rincón s/n, Yaiza, tel: 928 836 262, www.casonadeyaiza.com.* Eight attractively furnished rooms, heated pool and jacuzzi, good restaurant in the old wine cellar, gardens full of palms and cacti. The underground cisterns – *aljibes* – have become a small art gallery.

Finca de las Salinas €€€ (**€€€€** at Christmas/New Year) *Yaiza, tel: 928 830 325, www.fincasalinas.com.* A pink-washed country house, set in attactive gardens, on the road into Yaiza from the airport. There are 19 rooms, in buildings that used to be stables, decorated in earth shades and furnished with antiques. Pool, jacuzzi and sauna, views over Timanfaya Park.

Finca Malvasia €€–€€€ *Masdache, La Geria, tel: 692 155 981/ 665 468 538, www.fincamalvasia.com.* Four individually designed, whitewashed apartments with terraces are set in tastefully landscaped gardens around a pool in the heart of a working vineyard, with a backdrop of volcanic Timanfaya.

FUERTEVENTURA: PUERTO DEL ROSARIO

Hotel Fuerteventura Playa Blanca €€ *Playa Blanca, tel: 928 851 150.* This former parador stands alone, right on the beach between the capital and the airport. In a distinctive – if not beautiful – building, it offers excellent service and ocean views.

Puerto Rosario JM Palace €€ *Avenida Marítima 9, tel: 928 859 464, www.jmhoteles.com.* Opposite the port, this modern hotel has comfortable, air-conditioned rooms and friendly, obliging staff.

NORTHERN FUERTEVENTURA

CORRALEJO

Corralejo Beach Aparthotel € *Calle Victor Grau Bassas, tel: 928 866 315, www.corralejobeach.com.* Pleasant, functional one- and two-room apartments and two suites, close to the beach.

Riu Palace Tres Islas €€€ *Avenida Grandes Playas, tel: 928 535 700, www.riu.com.* Huge hotel, renovated in 2007, on the edge of the dunes, 5km (3 miles) from the town centre, with gym, tennis and all the facilities and comforts you would expect, indoors and out. Piano bar and children's daytime entertainment.

EL COTILLO/VILLAVERDE

Apartamentos La Gaviota €€ *Calle Betancourt 14, tel: 928 538 567.* This large white building sits in a garden close by the harbour; offers basic but comfortable accommodation in seven apartments.

Hotel Rural Mahoh €–€€ *Sitio Juan Bello s/n, Villaverde, La Oliva, tel: 928 868 050.* Early 19th-century house built of volcanic stone, with gardens, pool and multi-purpose sports pitch. Bedrooms furnished in traditional style. Environmentally-aware owners. Only about 10 minutes' drive from beaches of El Cotillo and Corralejo.

CENTRAL FUERTEVENTURA

CALETA DE FUSTES

Barceló Club El Castillo €€€ *Avenida El Castillo, tel: 928 163 101, www.barcelo.com.* This well-landscaped beach-side complex has pretty bungalows set in gardens; pools for adults and children, a children's playground and several restaurants. Terms can be self-catering, B&B, half-board or all-inclusive.

Casa Isaítas €€ *Calle Guize 7, Pájara, tel: 928 161 402, www. casaisaitas.com.* A delightful place, white-walled with Canarian balconies and a pretty courtyard. There is a good restaurant, and delicious breakfasts.

Suite Hotel Elba Castillo San Jorge €€ *Calle Franch y Roca s/n, tel: 928 163 500, www.hoteleselba.com.* About 500m/yds from the beach and the same distance from the town centre, this large aparthotel offers comfortable accommodation, in a complex with pools, sauna, restaurants and bars.

SOUTHERN FUERTEVENTURA

JANDÍA PLAYA

Barceló Jandía Playa €€€ *Calle La Mancha s/n, Barranco de Vinamar, tel: 928 546 000, www.barcelojandiaplaya.com.* Large hotel complex a few minutes from Morro del Jable. All modern comforts in an attractive setting, plus four pools, a gym, a solarium, a wellness centre, children's club, and four restaurants.

Hotel Meliá Gorriones €€€ *Playa la Barca, tel: 928 547 025, from UK: 0808-234 1953, www.solmelia.com.* In a quiet spot at the start of the Jandía Peninsula, this large hotel offers everything you need for a relaxed and comfortable beach holiday, and it is the base for the acclaimed René Egli Windsurf School. Minimum two-night stay.

Iberostar Playa Gaviotas Hotel €€€–€€€€ *Pasaje Playa 2, Jandía, tel: 928 166 197, www.iberostar.com.* Pleasant all-inclusive hotel right on the beach; air-conditioned rooms with terraces, restaurant, cocktail bar, two pools and children's pool. There are 16 family rooms and 6 rooms adapted for people with disabilities. The Iberostar chain has two other hotels in Jandía, the Fuerteventura Palace and the Playa Gaviotas Park *(see website above)*.

INDEX

Berlitz pocket g[uide]

Lanzarote & Fuerte[ventura]

Third Edition 2012
Reprinted 2015

Written and updated by Pam Barr[ett]
Commissioning Editor: Catherine [
Series Editor: Tom Stainer

Printed by CTPS – China

Berlitz Trademark Reg. U.S. Pat[
and other countries. Marca Reg[
Used under licence from the Ber[
Investment Corporation